BE YOU.
BE GREAT.

RITCHIE GIBSON

First Printed in 2015
by Inspire Trading Pty Ltd

The moral rights of the author have been asserted.

Author: Ritchie Gibson
Title: Be You. Be Great.

ISBN: 978-0-9944970-0-0

Cover design by Peter O'Connor – BespokeBookCovers.com

Cover photograph: Pamela Knox

What People have said about Ritchie Gibson and *Be You. Be Great.*

"Powerful messages and experiences delivered quickly. I love it.

This book will more than likely make you successful, if that's what you want, but it's certain to make you happier. That's what we all need!

I have led a charmed life, yet I still derive extreme value from these pages.

The best part though, is this can be my children's guide, because surely they won't all get my luck."

Ian Healy – Former ODI Australian Cricket Captain, Australian Cricket Hall of Fame inductee and Channel Nine broadcasting legend

If you want a better quality of life and to be a success, read this book, and then read it again.

This book will get you thinking differently and give you every chance of achieving your goals, both long and short term. "Go you Good thing."

Chris 'BUDDHA' Handy - Former Australian Wallaby Rugby Union player and Australian broadcasting legend.

This book, Be You. Be Great. is a must read if your a person that is trying too better themselves or just need some motivation. The more you read of this book the more confidence and belief you have that anything is possible. Congrats Ritchie and thanks for the inspiration.

Tonie Carroll - 4 Time NRL Premiership Winner with the Brisbane Broncos
Queensland, Australian and New Zealand Rugby League Representative

Ritchie Gibson first entered my life in 2000. At the time I was head coach of the Townsville Crocodiles in the National Basketball League, our season was on the brink, and we had lost star players with season-ending injuries. We had team chemistry issues with import players and were staring down a disastrous finish to the year.

We embarked on a team building, bonding, and challenging adventure with Ritchie, and it changed our season and fortune for the year. We went on a ten-game winning streak and made the NBL Grand Final for the first time in our franchise history.

While falling short of the ultimate season goal, I am certain our team achieved the best possible result for our group, and each player and coach was left with lifetime memories of our time with Ritchie. My coaching career has had a fair share of significant results with NBL and World Championship successes, and I hold the memories of my time with Ritchie in the same fondness as I do those results – the wins were great at the time, but Ritchie embedded strategies for dealing with adversity, creating resilience, and the value of teamwork and the importance of roles that will stay with me forever.

I'm glad to hear he has written a book; we need to learn from people like Ritchie who can change people's lives for the better.

IAN STACKER - Head Coach Townsville Crocodiles 1998-2005
NBL Coach of the Year 2000 & 2003
World Championship Gold Medal 1997 National Young Men's team
Head Coach Australian Institute of Sport Men 2010-2013

Dedication

This book is dedicated to the people – friends and family, both past and present – who have taught me life's lessons over the years.

You have made a contribution to the person I am today, and for that I thank you with all my heart. I can only hope there are many more lessons and life experiences to come.

I hope that this book provides inspiration and leaves a legacy for the next generation to build on.

> **"My close friends and family are the ones who know this book is from my heart. They are also the ones who will read it back to me when I have forgotten the words."**
> **– Ritchie Gibson, 2015**

About the Author

Ritchie Gibson grew up in housing commission and a working-class environment. His journey from inauspicious beginnings whilst witnessing alcohol and drug abuse and violence on a regular basis educated him not to be a victim of his circumstances and surroundings, but instead to learn from these crucial life lessons and to push himself to finding his passion in educating, inspiring, and motivating others.

Ritchie spent 12 years in the Australian Army and won awards and accreditations for outstanding service. He also received three military medals for active duty.

Now based in Brisbane in Queensland, Australia, he travels the country providing motivational and goal-setting solutions to corporate businesses, industry leaders, sports stars, and anyone who wants to improve their performance and is in need of motivation.

Table of Contents

Introduction

Every one of us spends countless hours considering our presents and planning our future. We all have some facet of our lives that we wish we could change or perhaps even more than one. Things like our health and fitness, family, relationships, work, and finances. The first step towards making these changes is to set goals.

While plenty of us are great at setting goals, many of us are practically incapable of following them through. If you are searching for a better quality of life, then it is up to you to follow through on your goals.

You have to do the work and the planning, and educate yourself on designing and building a happier life. This will occur only when you have a clear vision of what you want, how you intend to get it, and if you are not deterred or discouraged by the obstacles that life throws at you.

Once you have these ingredients, success becomes a matter of sticking to your plan and spending every day chipping away, and achieving the short-term goals required to get you to the long-term ones.

"Plan ahead. It wasn't raining when Noah built the Ark."
– Unknown

This book is written to help you realize that you have your own skill set – your own strong suit – and that you are more intelligent than you give yourself credit for.

Every expert started off as a rookie and had to learn the ropes. Every talent and skill – whether it is in finance, education, sports, music, or enterprise – can be learned.

Having definitive goals, a plan, and a burning desire to fulfill them is just the first step. This book will be your comprehensive guide to thinking differently, to having a successful and positive mindset, and to setting and fulfilling goals in each and every aspect of your life. It will make you think about why you are here and motivate you to be the best you can be.

I will share my life's experiences and what I believe are the key ingredients for you to become great regardless of your race, religion, gender, creed, or current education level. This book was written from the heart and will inject you with a dose of what I call GOYA, or "Get Off Your Ass."

Every single thing we do is controlled by our minds and our thought processes. This book is your long overdue mindset shift for the better.

"A goal without a plan is just a wish."
– Antoine de Saint-Exupery

Chapter 1: What Is Success?

"Preparation, hard work, taking action,
and learning from past failures are the
keys to success."
– Ritchie Gibson

How Badly do You Want It?

There once was a young man who wanted to make a lot of money and be successful. So he went to a guru and said, "I want to be at the same level as you are. I want to be rich. I want to be successful."

The guru replied, "If you want to be on the same level as me and be successful, meet me tomorrow at 4:00 a.m. at the beach."

The young man was clearly shocked and said, "The beach? You must have heard me wrong; I said I want to make money and be successful. I have no desire to learn how to swim."

The guru repeated, "If you want to be rich, if you want to be successful, then you'll meet me tomorrow at 4:00 a.m. at the beach."

The next morning, the young man arrived at the beach at the agreed hour. He was wearing a suit and tie and dressed to the nines, all the while thinking he should have worn shorts. The guru gently grabbed his hand and led him into the water and asked, "How badly do you want to be successful?"

The young man replied, "Really bad; more than anything."

The guru insisted that the young man walk deeper into the water, up to his waist. The young man started to question the guru and thought, **"This guy is crazy. I didn't ask to be a lifeguard. I want to make money and lots of it."**

The guru sensed the young man's anxiety and growing apprehension. He asked him to move out a little further. With the water now lapping up near their chins, they were on their tippy toes and barely able to touch the sand.

The guru then asked one more time, "How badly do you want to be successful?"

The young man replied, "More than anything."

With that, the guru placed his hand on the young man's head and pushed it under the water. The guru continued to hold down the young man, who scratched at the guru's arms and struggled to breathe and fought as hard as he could to return to the surface. The guru, sensing that the struggle had slowed and the young man was about to pass out, lifted him up.

When the young man had caught his breath, the guru spoke again.

"I've got a question for you," the guru said. "When you were underwater, what was the only thing you could think of and the only thing you wanted to do?"

The young man replied, "I wanted to breathe."

The guru then gave the young man the most valuable lesson he would ever learn. He told the young man, "When you want to succeed as badly as you want to breathe, then you'll be successful."

The Secret to Success

So, what is success?

Being a good parent? Being good at your job? Making lots of money?

The Oxford Dictionary defines success as "the accomplishment of an aim or purpose or the attainment of popularity or profit."

What that definition doesn't mention is the most important part of success: no matter what your endeavor, your desire and passion are the two things that will determine your success, not your aptitude or skill level.

Throughout my military career, I was fortunate enough to have worked with many determined and dedicated soldiers who truly epitomize mateship,[1] sacrifice, endurance, and courage. These are convictions that Australian troops pride themselves on, and they are things that set us apart from the rest of the world.

In 1999, I was deployed overseas on operations and was fortunate enough to work with a sergeant major who'd had a long and distinguished career. One day, the subject of success came up. I asked him his opinion on the difference between a Special Forces soldier and everyone else. What do Special Forces soldiers do that other soldiers don't?

He initially proceeded with a politically correct answer and said that it was their determination, never-say-die attitude, and strong mental state of mind.

I interrupted him and asked for his personal opinion and not something that just came out of a soldier's manual or something scripted. He gave me a look that could kill, but

---

1   i.e. brotherhood

then a small smirk appeared at the corner of his mouth. He rolled his eyes upward as if looking for a thought, then gave me his insightful answer.

He said, "Elite soldiers can deal with the boredom and monotony of training. They give their best every single day, even if they do the same thing over and over again. They are consistent day in and day out, and are committed to providing excellent service even on days when they don't feel like it."

> **"Successful people are simply those with successful habits."**
> **– Brian Tracy**

He stopped for a moment, but it was clear that he wasn't finished.

"Basically, an average soldier, when inspired or motivated, can perform at the top level for a while, but falls away after a few days or weeks and doesn't have the same consistency as the elite soldiers. Average soldiers become disillusioned when they fail or when an obstacle becomes too great. Once they lose their inspiration and desire to do their best, they tend to get disheartened and feel like they have lost momentum, which they find too difficult to get back. Most people think that the best soldiers have this unrelenting obsession and drive that others seem to be missing, but that is just not the case."

I pondered over this thought for a moment. I had always believed that too. Unrelenting obsession seemed like a prerequisite for being an elite soldier.

He continued, "But no! Elite soldiers experience the same lack of drive that everyone else feels. They don't have some magic formula that makes them feel ready and inspired every single day." He put his hand on my shoulder and looked me in the eye. "The difference," he said, "is that the best soldiers persist with their goals because they don't allow their emotions to influence their actions. They consistently, whether they feel like it or not, find a way to do the small, mundane, and boring things needed to achieve their goals. This ability to train, work, and do the hard yards regardless of who is paying attention is the difference between an elite soldier and everyone else."

> **"Success is the sum of small efforts – repeated day in and day out."**
> **– Robert Collier**

Internal vs. External

The elite are willing to work at a greater level of intensity because they are **internally** motivated, not **externally** motivated.

What's the difference, I hear you ask?

A soldier who plays sports, keeps fit, or works for recognition, material rewards, praise, medals, or personal status is externally motivated. But if the soldier participates because he enjoys the activity and wants to accomplish something for his self-worth and self-fulfillment, then he is internally motivated.

A great guide to differentiating between internal and external motivation is how a person feels after he or she has achieved something. If you feel satisfied **only** after you win or finish at the top, then you are externally motivated. But if you can feel satisfied by knowing deep within yourself how hard you have trained, and if you are not concerned whether you win or lose as long as you have given your all, then you are internally motivated. The bottom line is that internal motivation means you derive satisfaction from achieving instead of from external rewards.

The lesson I learned was that if you want to be successful at anything, consistency is the key – and that means training, educating, and pushing yourself even when the will is not there and boredom has set in. If you understand this, then over time success will come out in the wash.

> **"Some things you have to do every day. Eating seven apples on Saturday night instead of one a day just isn't going to get the job done."**
> **– Jim Rohn**

My Takeaway for this chapter:

Just remember, it takes ten years to become an overnight success. Chipping away day by day and forcing yourself to do the little things well is the key to long-term success. Don't let the boredom or lack of willpower stop you. Do it anyway.

Being successful is not about reaching a goal; it's about knowing you have done the best you can do regardless of the outcome.

Chapter 2: Fall Seven Times, Stand Up Eight

Strength doesn't come from what you can
do. It comes from overcoming the things
you once thought you couldn't.
– Rikki Rogers

One Foot in Front of the Other

I was doing an intensive army training course and was having a conversation with a friend. I told him that I was concerned about not performing my best and that I kept thinking, "What if I don't make it through?"

He turned to me, frowning, eyes squinting in confusion, and gave a slight shake of the head.

I repeated, "You know, what happens if I fall down, get knocked out, pass out, or just collapse through complete exhaustion? What happens if I can't make it?"

His reply is something that I will never forget.

He said, "I don't get it. If you fall down, collapse, or pass out, eventually you will wake back up. When you do, you stand up, put one foot in front of the other, and keep going. You repeat the process until you get the job done.

"If you're determined, you are not fazed or deterred by failure. Determination is perseverance in spite of obstacles that are put in front of you. It's as simple as that!"

What my friend was trying to say was that success comes down to your level of determination and commitment. Put simply, whether you achieve success depends on how badly you want it! If you are determined and deeply focused on achieving your goals, then nothing can stop you.

> **"You've got to get up every morning with determination if you are going to go to bed with satisfaction."**
> **– George Lorimer**

Determination Determines Your Destination

Determination means having your mind made up or set regarding a decision. When you find yourself in a compromising situation, in your mind, there aren't any options or decisions to make; you already know what to do.

Determination is not just a feeling. There is a "will" element involved as well – a strong emotional state that drives you to change your present position into something better. Determination provides an unrelenting mental clarity about the line of action you take. When you have determination, you emanate an aura of confidence, boldness, and hunger that is difficult to explain.

Perseverance is the starting point of what makes a successful person. It is closely related to and shares the same DNA as determination. If you want to be successful in life, understand that you only ever succeed at anything because you are determined to succeed, not because you are destined to succeed.

It is impossible to be successful if you don't have determination. Determination is what gives you the strength and grit to get through the most difficult of obstacles. I stay determined by not allowing my mind to even consider that my goals won't be achieved. The moment doubt creeps in and you allow your mind to devise an alternative plan, you have subconsciously given up on your initial goal. I stick with Plan A and make the extra effort to get it done. The thing that separates the winners and successful people from any ordinary person is not talent, but effort.

Look at the stonecutter hammering away at his rock, perhaps a hundred times without as much as a crack showing in it. Yet at the hundred and first blow it will split in two, and I know it was not the last blow that did it, but all that had gone before.
– Jacob August Riis

Brick Walls

If you are in control of your life, you can do anything.

When I was taking structured lessons and instructing younger soldiers on ethics training and the importance of mental toughness in the face of adversity, I would approach a brick wall and bang my hand against it. I would then tell the audience that I could walk through this wall.

A large percentage of people have the mentality of, **"It's a brick wall! You won't get through that!"**

But I know that with persistence and determination, I will eventually get through the wall. I am aware that it won't happen overnight and that I will be faced with obstacles and sacrifices, but eventually, as long as I have obsessive determination and a burning desire to succeed, I will get through the wall.

The brick wall is a metaphor for anything in life that serves as a challenge or obstacle. If our passion and desires are strong enough, we can achieve anything.

"The brick walls are there for a reason. The brick walls are not there to keep us out. The brick walls are there to give us a chance to show how badly we want something. Because the brick walls are there to stop the people

> **who don't want it badly enough. They're there**
> **to stop the other people."**
> **– Randy Pausch**

It is surprising to see how many people don't fully understand the difference between desperation and determination. Desperation means making rash decisions when options are limited or choices are few. When a person is desperate, he or she will do almost anything necessary to ensure short-term happiness. Alternatively, a determined person will not settle for anything less than his or her perceived and desired outcome.

Just one step away from desperation is the energy of determination. Take that step, and put all that energy to good use.

> **"I believe that the only people on this planet**
> **with a disability are those who do not believe**
> **in themselves and lack the determination to**
> **improve their life."**
> **– Ritchie Gibson**

What Motivates You?

In 2007, I was working overseas when I met a man named Al Marco. Al is a self-made multimillionaire who had a bumpy road to success. He was diagnosed at an early age with dyslexia and was bullied through the majority of his schooling years. His challenging situation pushed him to succeed and prove all his doubters wrong. Al was able to take adversity and turn it into a reason to be better. I remember one particular day, we were playing golf and Al asked me, "Where do you see yourself in five years' time?"

I replied, "That's an easy one. I'll be semi-retired. I'll be playing golf, fishing, presenting, and living a life that I want to live."

"You'll be semi-retired?" he inquired.

"Yeah," I answered with no hesitation.

He replied, "I am comfortable and what most would consider wealthy. My children, even my grandchildren will never have to work a day in their entire lives if they don't want to. However, I would hope they find the same joy in the ability to work and create, and not see money as the motivation.

"I've got two young children at home that I love spending time with. So, why do I get up early every single morning and work between 50-60 hours per week? Because I'm not motivated by the money; I'm motivated by the challenge."

This really resonated with me. I found myself asking the question, "What really motivates me – the money or the challenge?"

It's really important you realize money is not a motivator – it is just a means to an end, a way of getting you to where you want to go. As discussed in Chapter 1, external influences such as money, power, and fame are insignificant compared to a true passion for what you do.

Over time, motivation has to be the challenge. It includes the goal in your head, the distinct plan you have created, and how you're going to accomplish that plan.

My Takeaway for this chapter:

Just remember that you can do anything. The obstacles and roadblocks in life are thrown at us to see how badly we want something. These obstacles are put before us to stop the people who don't have as strong a will as you do. They are there to stop others, not you.

What really motivates people isn't always money, but the want to do the right thing every day and the challenges that come with it."

Chapter 3: When Nothing Goes Right, Go Left

"Luck is where preparation meets opportunity."
– Seneca

You Make Your Own Luck

On various occasions, I have heard people say "You are really lucky!" or "You have luck on your side!"

I am quite shocked that people believe that some individuals have a lot of luck on their side and others do not. I don't believe in luck; I believe in life. Life is a precious gift, a gift you are throwing away when you believe that it depends on luck or good fortune.

In reality, people get lucky because they are focused, they want something badly enough, and they put in a lot of hard work to achieve their goals.

> **"I'm a great believer in luck, and I find the harder I work, the more I have of it."**
> **– Thomas Jefferson**

You need to eradicate the word "luck" from your mind. Once you have, you will start to realize that life is what you make it. No one can determine whether you are lucky or unlucky except you. You create every moment in your life.

Sometimes things go the way you've planned, and sometimes they don't. However, this is not determined by luck. More often than not, when something I perceived as a bad thing has happened to me, it has turned out to be a blessing in disguise.

> **"Sometimes things fall apart so that better things can fall together."**
> **– Marilyn Monroe**

When Things Fall Apart

We have all experienced bad days; and at times, especially on our worst days, we may have almost convinced ourselves that the world is going to end. Remember, though: it's just a bad day, not a bad life.

> **"Sadness is almost never anything but
> a form of fatigue."
> – Andre Gide**

It could have started with an argument that led to a relationship breakup, with being sacked from your job, a car accident, or a financial loss that depleted everything you've worked hard for. Whatever it was that knocked you on your backside and devastated you to your core may well have been a blessing in disguise.

In my opinion, the reason why controlling your state of mind and your perceptions is the most important thing in life to master is that doing so allows you to appreciate that every negative experience you're going through is part of the grand plan and will lead you toward achieving your goals.

This is difficult to get your head around, and it takes work. But by trying to find the good in every situation and by having faith that an obstacle or setback is necessary for you to achieve your vision and happiness, the less disappointed and discouraged you will feel.

Unforeseen setbacks can lead to new and positive opportunities. If you can perceive that your cup is half full and not half empty, you can find fulfillment in every situation.

If you want to be successful and find greatness in your life, controlling your perceptions and how you deal with every experience must be your number one priority.

If you believe that everyone and everything comes into your life for a reason – some for good, some for bad – and that each one shapes you to be the person you are today, you will begin to identify every experience, no matter how much of an obstacle it seems to be, as a possibility for growth and progression in your life.

Two examples of how a changed perception can impact your life:

1. Back in 2012, I decided to write a journal for my wife. Every day for almost twelve months, I wrote something positive about her and the reasons I loved her. I looked for the small things she did, which I tended to take for granted, rather than her bigger and more obvious qualities. I looked for the qualities and reasons why I fell in love with her in the first place. I gave the journal to her for Christmas that year, and she cried and said it was the most thoughtful gift that anyone had ever given her.

Here's the kicker, though: the person that the journal had the greatest emotional impact on was **me**.

Research suggests that when a human being expresses kindness and appreciation to another human being, it raises the serotonin[2] levels in both people's brains. Gratitude physiologically makes us feel better.

Although I invested fewer than five minutes on it every day, the journal made me focus on my wife's positive aspects. I noticed that I was consciously looking for all her positives – and, due to this perception and mindset

2   A neurotransmitter is thought to contribute to feelings of well-being and happiness.

change, I was seeing the subtleties in her nature and behavior.

By looking for the positive qualities in your partner and changing your perceptions, you change your view of them, which in turn changes the way you interact with them. Seeing first-hand how this perception impacted my relationship and believing that other people would be experiencing the same difficulties we'd had, a friend and I decided to start a business. I named the business TWILY, an acronym that stands for "That's Why I Love You." TWILY is a journal designed to be filled out by one partner and given to the other.[3]

2. December 21, 2012 marked the completion of the Great Mayan Cycle and the beginning of a New World Age. By focusing too heavily on the negativity in the press and media, you may be missing the true significance of this ominous date – the date on which, according to the Mayan prophecy, the world would end.

We are constantly bombarded with negatives, fear, and the premise that something bad is never too far away. If it's not terrorism, it's violence, politics, or something else that creates anxiety and stress.

How would it make you feel and how would it change your perceptions if the date suggested above was not the end of the world, but instead of the beginning of a bright new future for mankind and humanity – a future that allowed us to be conscious of realizing our real potential as human beings? What if your thought process and belief was that strong, you were convinced that this date, instead of the end of the world, meant a fresh start for everyone, the starting date for people to reach their true potential?

---

3   www.twily.com

That's the power of perceptions and controlling your state of mind.

> **"Your perception of anyone, including yourself, is not the truth. The truth is buried somewhere underneath what your parents, teachers, schoolmates, even what you told yourself from birth to this moment."**
> **– Amy Larson**

My Takeaway for this chapter:

Our perceptions stem from our beliefs. As we grow older, our beliefs change and so too do our perceptions. A good question to ask yourself is 'Am I a victim here, or the Victor?'

Sometimes, when something bad happens, your personal trajectory can change in an incredible way, and for the better.

Chapter 4: What You Perceive, You Believe

"Everything we hear is an opinion, not a fact.
Everything we see is a perspective, not the truth."
– Marcus Aurelius

The Power of Perspective!

Life's all about how you approach it. How you control what you think about is the single most important thing you should try to master.

The only person who can ultimately affect or control your state of mind is you, so make sure that you utilize this power to direct your mindset and make it conducive to your dreams and goals.

You experience this world only through the perceptions that you create. You have the ability to choose how you perceive any event in your life, and you exercise this power of choice in every circumstance every day. No matter what the situation, you choose your reaction and assign meaning and value to each event.

> **"The same boiling water that softens potatoes hardens eggs. It's all about what you are made of, not your circumstances."**
> **– Unknown**

We all view the world through individual filters that influence the interpretations we give events, how we respond, and how we are responded to. Be aware of the factors that influence the way you see the world, so you can compensate for them and react against them. If you continue to view the world through a filter created by past events, then you are allowing your past to control and dictate both your present and your future.

Filters are made up of fixed beliefs and negative ideas that have become entrenched in your thinking. They are dangerous because if you treat them as fact, you will not seek, receive, or process new information. This undermines your plans for change. If you shake up your belief system by challenging your views and testing their validity, the freshness of your perspective can be startling.

Just because we see something in a particular way does not make it so. We can be so insistent sometimes that our way of seeing something is more right than someone else's view.

**"We can complain because rose bushes have thorns,
or rejoice because thorn bushes have roses."
– Abraham Lincoln**

Keep an open mind at all times and remember that each individual's point of view is always valuable to that individual.

What you see as real is defined by your belief structure. Your version of what is real is only your perception of reality.

Here's an example: Let's say somebody in your family died. (I use this example because it's something I've been through. Both my parents died within 9 months of each other and it was an extremely difficult period of my life. The hurt, immense pain and emotions you feel seem like they will never subside.) You have the choice though, about how you respond to that death. You can choose to see it as something terrible and tragic or as something that inspires you to make more of your life.

After a time of grieving, sometimes this can take years, if not decades, we will still dearly miss the people we lose, but we have the choice of how to respond to that loss. We can dwell on losing the person, or we can be thankful for the time we had with them and be inspired to live our lives fully.

From that example, you can see that although you may or may not have control over the events in your life, you can certainly take control of how to respond to them. That part of life will always be within your power.

This is where life gets interesting, because you shape your reality through your beliefs.

Your belief structure determines your perception, which ultimately controls how you respond to events. Going by that sequence, you can see that the way to change your perception is to examine your beliefs and then choose to change them. Everything begins with a choice.

Most of our beliefs are held not because we have verified them for ourselves, but for many other different reasons. Those reasons range from the influence of our environment in childhood to the influence of the media in adult life.

Remember that what you believe to be true is only as true as your worldly experience; your reality doesn't go any further than that. In the end, what really matters is exactly the conclusion you draw.

We all approach the world with our own set of perceptions shaped by who we are and who we have been. Being tolerant of and open-minded to how others' perceptions differ from our own can widen our experiences and perceptions and provide possibilities for growth and discovery.

> **"Holding a grudge is letting someone live rent-free in your head."**
> **– Unknown**

You are Who You Surround Yourself With

You cannot spend time with negative people and expect to have a positive life. The late American entrepreneur, author, and motivational speaker Jim Rohn put it best when he said, "You are the average of the five people you spend the most time with." So choose carefully. Make sure the people you spend most of your time with don't bring you down.

When they see you changing, growing, and developing into a better person, negative people will try to bring you down because they fear that you are going to outgrow them. They have to make themselves feel better by putting you down because they lack the determination and willpower to do what you are doing. Quite often, people who criticize your life don't know or understand the price you paid and sacrifices you made to get where you are today.

One of the best pieces of advice I have ever received was from my brother. I was angry and frustrated with someone, and my brother told me not to rent the space out in my head to someone or something that meant so little to me. He said that the most valuable real estate you own is between your ears, so don't let cheap people rent it out.

Distance yourself from these types of people, and stay positive. Look for positive people to associate with. Always ponder how you can, not why you can't.

> **"Keep away from people who try to belittle
> your ambitions. Small people always do that,
> but the really great make you feel that you,
> too, can become great."**
> **– Mark Twain**

My Takeaway for this chapter:

Your thoughts have an imaginative factor to them. Regardless how small that thought or belief is, be aware that you are always creating whenever you think. We all should recognize that our beliefs are decisions. We make that choice. Therefore, we create our own reality.

Surround yourself with people that not only make you happy, but make you want to be a better person.

Chapter 5: Happiness is a Choice, Not a Response

"Beware of destination addiction...

A preoccupation with the idea that
happiness is in the next place, the next job,
or with the next partner. Until you give up
the idea that happiness is somewhere else,
it will never be where you are. "
– Lauren Britt

Happiness Is a Choice

I spent 12 months not exercising and being an observer in life instead of a participant. I was doing something that didn't inspire me to be the best I could be. I was talked into someone else's dream, and by the time I realized I was helping someone else live their dream and build their goals, I had committed too much time and money to turn back – or so I thought.

I believed that the years I had dedicated to a certain business project and the investment I made financially and more importantly, time-wise, needed a reward or a pot of gold at the end to justify chasing someone else's dream and not having to admit that I had failed at something.

> **"If you fail, never give up because F.A.I.L.**
> **means 'First Attempt in Learning.'"**
> **– Unknown**

I felt flat, depressed, and in a rut. I felt myself become negative towards most things, and I could feel excuses starting to dictate and rule my life. I had an underlying fear that this was how the rest of my life was going to be.

I tried different things to compensate for the way I was feeling, but at the end of the day, I was in that state of mind because I wasn't fulfilling my passion. I was living and working a life that someone had told me was the right thing for me instead of listening to my gut instinct and intuition and doing what I loved.

I became distant from friends, and would say things were going good and never elaborate further on my life or how I was feeling. I felt that I was no longer an influence on others; I no longer inspired people, and I no longer inspired myself!

I was far from rock bottom – I just didn't feel fulfilled at that time, and life was passing me by. I have never wanted that. I have always wanted to get to the end of my life and know that I achieved everything I set out to do. I don't want to have any regrets.

It doesn't take much to lose your momentum in life, especially when the choices you have made are the reason behind your stagnation. You start to lose momentum when you get lazy or decide to give up.

When you realize that certain expectations or goals were not achieved and you are not yet where you want to be in life, you can either give up and lose momentum, or you can change.[4]

When this happened to me, I made a mental line in the sand and told myself that as of right now, things had to change.

> **"We don't rise to the level of our abilities;**
> **we fall to the level of our excuses."**
> **– Peter James**

The Line in the Sand

I was at the point of "enough is enough"; things needed to change. I was sick and tired of my current lifestyle and behaviors and needed to muster up the strength, motivation, and desire needed to change and become a better version of my current self.

Change is difficult and brings uncertainties. Most of us subconsciously do not change; staying the same is a way of protecting ourselves from things that we're unsure of. This can be both a blessing and a curse.

---

4   We'll talk about momentum more in the next chapter.

The famous Australian pop diva Kylie Minogue once wrote a song called "Better the Devil You Know." This song always reminds me that most of us would rather live with our old habits, no matter how bad they make us feel or how frustrated we are with them, just because they are familiar.

I needed to refocus my energy away from being unhappy and knew that a good night's sleep was a great starting point.

I remember setting the alarm for 4:45 a.m. so I could watch the sunrise. I was on vacation with my wife. Where we were staying, it was only a 10-minute walk from the beach. I told my wife my intention, and she laughed at me – and rightly so. The previous 12 months, I had said I was going to do a lot of things, and only a few of those things came to fruition. She had every right to be skeptical and think that I would sleep in as I had previously.

After being stuck in a rut for a full year, I jumped out of bed when my alarm went off and headed for the beach. No more than 100 yards past the door to our room, I found a $10 note sitting in the middle of the path. Something told me that was a sign of good things to come.

I arrived at the beach and watched the sunrise. I remembered being in awe of the moment. I felt that I had arrived at the start of the rest of my life. I knew there and then that the past 12 months – the bad attitude, the depression, and the thoughts of treading water – were over. I had turned a corner and made a conscious decision to get off my backside and out of the rut and to start focusing on the positives and the person I wanted to be.

There would be no more excuses, and more importantly, I found myself believing again in what I knew I was capable of. I sat on the beach for two hours, and I can tell you without a shadow of a doubt that my entire life changed in that two-hour period. It was majestic.

That's when I truly realized how important state of mind and perceptions are. There is absolutely nothing more crucial in creating a successful life for yourself. Nothing.

"Defeat is a state of mind; no one is ever defeated until defeat has been accepted as reality."
– Bruce Lee

I had taught for years that health had to be the number one priority. I used to ask people what the number one priority in their lives was. Some people would say their wife, kids, house, cars, or money. When I got those answers, I would ask, "Where would all those things be if you didn't have your health?" For years, I truly believed that your health should be your number one priority, but that day on the beach changed my mind. How you control your state of mind and your perceptions – how you see things – is more important.

Most people don't realize why they are here, why they are alive. Every single human being is on this earth for a reason. Many people think that they can't make a difference – that because they are not in a powerful position or don't have a great deal of money, they are not able to influence others.

I always felt like I was on the verge of starting something. For many years, I felt that the life I wanted was about to begin, but there were always obstacles in my way. There were debts to be paid and unfinished business to attend to and an in-tray to empty. I kept thinking that as soon as I got them out of the way, I could start my new life and be happy.

Then it dawned on me that these obstacles **were** my life. And at that point, I made a decision to be happy, not to wait for happiness. I realized that happiness is not rooted in events, purchases, or special occasions. It is a decision, a state of mind, and an attitude.

We don't need wealth, notoriety, or the body of an Adonis. What we need is to use our minds. That is everything we need to achieve happiness.

Time and tide wait for no man. Make sure you treasure each and every moment you have been given. If you find yourself in a rut, get a good night's sleep and start fresh with exercise or watching the sunrise.

Happiness Is Not a Destination, but a Way of Life

Of the 7.3 billion people on this planet, one thing we all have in common is that we all strive for one simple thing: **happiness**.

But what is happiness? What is this amazing and sometimes elusive emotion that we're all chasing after?

Happiness comes in many different forms. Most of us experience happiness at some time in our lives because of a wedding, the birth of a child, the purchase of the house of our dreams, or even a job promotion.

> **"What a wonderful thought it is that some of the best days of our lives haven't happened yet!"**
> **– Unknown**

Despite this, characterizing genuine happiness is tough to do – just as hard as it is to attain. So what we need to do is to distinguish amongst moments of pleasure, feelings of elation, and actual happiness.

In the Western world, we are born into a society of wants and needs and think that once we get what we want and what we have being striving for, we will then be happy. Our culture is based on buying our way to happiness, with feelings of satisfaction strongly influenced by judging ourselves against others and what they have. This only leads to a desire for more and more, which in turn leads to resentment, frustration, and disappointment.

Some material things are important and essential for a more comfortable life, but they are not the key to developing long-term contentment and happiness.

I have a close friend who has pretty much everything he wants – a lifestyle most people would envy. He mentioned to me that he was now happy in his occupation, as he'd just received a promotion and a pay raise; however, that happiness was short-lived. Soon enough, he was miserable again.

> **"The secret to happiness is doing what you love,
> and the secret to success is loving what you do."
> – Vanny Angel**

Finding Happiness

Finding happiness solely through career aspirations is always going to be a difficult way to maintain happiness, as it is a moving target. It is human nature to want more. Once you get that promotion, pay raise, or corner office, it does not take you long to start thinking of how happier you will be when you reach the next level – and the cycle perpetuates.

That doesn't mean that one should not be ambitious and strive for a promotion or a greater salary or wage. What it means is that only fleeting happiness can come from achieving a goal you have set for yourself. Happiness isn't about doing; happiness is about being.

A good example is this: every single astronaut who took part in the Apollo 11 lunar mission back in 1969 returned home with some form of depression. They had accomplished their lifelong goals and felt that anything else they did in life would fall short of that accomplishment.

> **"What does a man do for an encore after that?"**
> **– Buzz Aldrin**

This is because once you achieve the goal and vision you have set for yourself, once you've reached your life-long achievement and are living the life you dreamed of, that life is suddenly not enough anymore. As human beings, we need growth. After we've achieved a goal, we'll want something bigger and better and will concoct another vision to chase after and be happy about.

I think that a major contributing factor to long-term happiness is perceived growth and continued self-improvement. You need to perceive that you are growing, giving, and making a difference to your life. The sensation of moving forward and progressing in health, travel, fitness, career, family, relationships, education, and spirituality will lead to a happier and more fulfilling life.

Happiness Is Also About Giving and Sharing with Others

Imagine that you went to a stadium and watched the Super Bowl, the Football World Cup final or a famous rock concert. If you had the best seats in the house and were surrounded by more than 100,000 screaming fans, the atmosphere would be electric. It would feel truly unbelievable, and you would be happy simply because you were sharing it with other people.

But now imagine you were the only spectator. The stadium would have a hollow and empty mood with no noise and no euphoric atmosphere. You would probably struggle to enjoy the game.

An internal conflict arises and becomes challenging when you have to make a choice between something that will provide short-term pleasure and something that will deliver long-term happiness. A lot of the time, it is when we make choices to abstain from short-term pleasure that we inch closer to long-term happiness.

A good way to decide if something will provide you with long-term happiness or short-term satisfaction is by asking yourself, "Will this **actually** make me happy in the long run?"

I often hear people talk about their love of using retail therapy when they are down and in need of a little pick-me-up. However, recent research suggests that unhappiness and being pessimistic are linked with a materialistic mindset.

People who "buy" happiness find themselves still unhappy. The simple reason for this is that although material things bring pleasure for a period of time, pleasure is inconsistent and has no guarantee of being there tomorrow. It can be in abundance one day and potentially gone the next, whereas happiness is with you all the time.

The same research shows that people who decide to relinquish and decrease their purchases and materialistic lifestyles free themselves from debt and become happier through a simpler and less complicated life.

> **"Thousands of candles can be lighted from a single candle, and the life of the candle will not be shortened. Happiness never decreases by being shared."**
> **– Buddha**

Happiness Comes from We not Me.

Having a materialistic mindset and wanting to buy more to be happy is a diversion from what actually does make people happy, which is developing relationships and pursuing passions. One form of happiness is achieved from creating strong bonds and connections with people and by giving and assisting others, which allows us to fill an emotional and spiritual need we all long for.

The reason behind this is that happiness comes from **we** (the generosity and compassion shown to other human beings) and not **me** ("I want this" and "I want that" and "I will only be happy when I achieve this").

Denmark has been declared the happiest nation in the world and the happiest country in Europe every year since 1973. So what are the Danish doing that the rest of the Western world is not?

The Danish attribute their well-being and happiness primarily to a) the generosity and kindness of their population, b) strong relationships, and c) community support programs that encourage people to design mental pictures of happiness in every aspect of their lives.

If you are happy in one area of your life, it is probably because you are in sync with the vision that you originally created for yourself. This means that your happiness is closely related to the expectations you have set for your life and how you perceive things should be.

"Remember, happiness doesn't depend upon who you are or what you have; it depends solely upon what you think."
– Dale Carnegie

If your vision and mental picture of what you wanted for your life does not match where you are right now, this can lead to unhappiness and a feeling of failure.

If your goals are to be slim and fit and to maintain a healthy lifestyle, but you see yourself as overweight, it is your perception and expectation that are making you unhappy.

A sumo wrestler is happy to be overweight because that is what he strives for; however, a normal person in Western culture may not be happy being overweight – because being overweight is not part of the vision he or she had for him- or herself; nor is it what society dictates is ideal.

Once you realize and value your happiness as more than a goal – and once you realize you are more than the story or vision you have made up in your head – then you will be on your way to happiness. If you're not happy, you need to change the picture you have in your mind.

"Change is inevitable. Growth is optional."
– John C. Maxwell

One of the first steps is to define your version of happiness and simplicity. What does this vision look like? When I started to simplify my life, I asked myself three big questions:

1. "What makes me happy?"

2. "Am I honestly trying to compete with others? Even on a subconscious level?"

3. "How can I simplify my life to enhance my happiness?"

   "When I was 5 years old, my mother always told me that happiness was the key to life. When I went to school, they asked me what I wanted to be when I grew up. I wrote down 'happy.' They told me I didn't understand the assignment, and I told them they didn't understand life."
   – John Lennon

My Takeaway for this chapter:

If you are not happy and feel unfulfilled, ask yourself if it is because of one particular aspect of your life. If it is, change your visual image and expectation of "how it should be." True happiness comes from your state of mind and your attitude towards life.

Don't get hung up on retail therapy and buying happiness. Material possessions are only a Band-Aid treatment and a short-term fix, not a long-term solution to lasting happiness.

Happiness isn't about doing. Happiness is about being.

Happiness comes from We, not Me.

Chapter 6: The Secret to Getting Ahead is Getting Started

"The man who removes a mountain
begins by carrying away small stones."
– Chinese proverb

The Power of Momentum

It is odorless, colorless, and tasteless. You can feel it, lose it, and gain it. It's elusive, it's invisible, and at times it's difficult to find. But when you have it, you are well on your way to achieving your goals. It is something that all elite soldiers, athletes, and successful people possess, and it's called the power of momentum. Momentum is one of the greatest examples of the Law of Attraction at work.

You hear it all the time – "I'm on a roll," "I should buy a lottery ticket," – when everything just seems to go according to plan. This could be in any aspect of life: money, relationships, career, or health and fitness. Unfortunately, all good things must come to an end, and momentum eventually stops. This is normally brought on by some sort of adversity or obstacle.

But what if you didn't take any notice of the obstacles life threw at you and decided your roll wouldn't end? What if you decided and had a strong enough mindset that having momentum continuously was just the way your life was?

Creating momentum in your life is not that difficult, but most of us are not aware of how to consciously achieve it.

So what is momentum? Without getting too scientific, and in layman's terms, momentum would be best described as: if something is moving, it is said to have momentum.

So why do so few people in this day and age find it hard to gain momentum? I believe it is due to our newfound sedentary lifestyle, where sitting in front of a computer, laptop, or tablet and texting, watching TV, gaming, driving, etc. leave most of us with zero momentum. Maybe it's because we're moving less and not getting anywhere.

Momentum is more than just moving. Momentum is a mindset shift. It is a satisfying sense of progression that gives your life energy, encouragement, and that get-up-and-go attitude.

Chipping away and working toward your goals is the best way to build momentum. With time and persistence, every step and decision you make will get easier as you go along. You will start to enjoy every aspect of your life; you will have more self-belief and confidence because you have momentum on your side!

The first and probably most important step is to get started. By starting something, you will rise above inactivity and overcome your lack of movement with action. Affirming, strategizing, preparing, wishing, hoping, dreaming, and the like will not build momentum. Momentum requires movement.

> **"The most important thing you can do to achieve your goals is to make sure that as soon as you set them, you immediately begin to create momentum."**
> **– Tony Robbins**

The Importance of Short-Term Goals

Ease yourself into it if you have to, and take small steps at first if necessary. Having short-term goals is a good starting point, because your enthusiasm for achieving small goals will begin to compound and have a snowball effect with your long-term ones.

Where a lot of people go wrong is in setting unrealistically large goals in the beginning. Just the thought of such a large mountain to climb is off-putting.

Many goals are discarded because people take action and make an effort, wait to see what the results are, and then quit when they don't see the results they expected. Don't get sucked into this train of thought and become so fixated on results that you get discouraged. I have seen this time and time again with people wanting to lose weight: when the scales don't tell them what they want to hear, they become disheartened and lose any momentum they may have gained. Just concentrate on keeping the ball rolling, even if you're not seeing the results you want. If you get discouraged and quit, you're guaranteed not to see any results. Concentrate on building momentum.

Once you have momentum, you will be able to feel or sense it. It is then important to maintain it; when you do, it will get easier to keep going. Believe that if you keep putting in the effort and work hard at something every day, your momentum will grow. One classic indicator of momentum is that as it grows, things get easier and you need to put forth less effort to achieve the same results.

"Action alone is the timber that ignites momentum."
– Ritchie Gibson

How Do You Eat an Elephant? One Bite at a Time!

On your journey to a successful and fulfilling life, you need to determine exactly what it is you want. To achieve this, you will require a detailed plan and the determination to work at it every day.

Don't set out to build the Great Wall of China. Aiming for something so enormous almost always ends in total failure. Instead, think about it this way: set your mind to laying down one brick at a time, and then another. If you do that every day, before you know it, you'll have a wall. This is how you should set goals in life – one brick at a time.

Achieve something small every day and work gradually to bigger and bigger goals. When you set lifetime goals, think about what you can do every day to achieve them. A daily list of things to do can help you set up the bricks.

The first step is simple: think about what you want to achieve. Once it is clear to you, the rest of the decision-making process will be easy. Start with the end in mind and work back from there.

> **"A year from now,
> you will wish you had started today."
> – Karen Lamb**

Finding Your Blueprint

A contractor cannot build a good house without a blueprint or detailed set of plans. Neither can a pilot expect to arrive safely at his destination without a flight plan, map coordinates, and a strategy of how he is going to get there. Establishing goals in every facet of your life is no different.

First, understand that there are no limits to what you can achieve. This may be difficult to comprehend, but it's true.

Second, if you could have anything you wanted in every facet of your life – such as health, relationships, work, sports, finance – what would that look like?

Third, you need to understand that the buck stops with you. You need to be accountable for every choice and decision you make and not accept **any** excuses. Until you get this aspect right, nothing will change. If changing your life means everything to you, you will find a way. If not, you will find an excuse.

> **"Determination is the process which drives perseverance. But to start the engine, you first require commitment."**
> **– Ritchie Gibson**

Some people are so adept at making excuses that they make them automatically or subconsciously. They constantly attempt to avoid responsibility for choices or decisions they make. **When faced with making a choice or offering an excuse, take responsibility and ownership for your actions.** Consider for a minute if avoiding the blame is worth jeopardizing your self-respect and the respect others have for you. Do you want to be known as the person who has the courage to take responsibility for your actions or the person who always has an excuse?

As we grow up, our lives become accumulations of all the choices or decisions we make. You are reading this book, but before you began, you made the decision to buy it, and then you made another choice to read it.

Everything in your life exists because you first made a choice about something.

Choices develop into habits. Every decision you make in some shape or form will alter the path you take in life.

No one began their life with everything they needed to succeed. No one is better than you are. Every skill someone has – in business, communication and negotiation, relationships – that person learned over the course of a lifetime. Everyone who is good in any area today was once poor in that area. Experts begin not even knowing their field exists. Hundreds of thousands of people around the globe have risen to the top of their fields. You can do so too.

Write down your goals. Be sure to make them specific and detailed, and the progress you make on them measurable. Less than 5% of the world's population takes the time to have written goals and a vision board of some description, and coincidently, the remaining 95% of people work for them.

> **"If you don't build your dream,**
> **someone else will hire you to build theirs."**
> **– Tony Gaskins**

My Takeaway for this chapter:

How do you build momentum?

First: start moving and move in the direction of your goals.

Second: take action.

Third: make no excuses and don't give in to obstacles or adversity.

Fourth: if you fall and your momentum starts to dwindle, get back up and go until you feel it come back.

Fifth: only when things start to appear to get fractionally easier will you know you have started to build momentum and you're getting your mojo back.

Chapter 7: The Importance of Goals and High Standards

"Never apologize for having high
standards. People who really want to be in
your life will rise up to meet them."
– Ziad K. Abdelnour

Keep Your Head and Your Standards High

Now that you understand that everything in your life is a result of the choices and decisions you make, you need to decide what standards you are going to live by. If your life is not how you envisaged it, maybe it is time to start raising your standards by making better decisions.

Having higher standards does not mean comparing yourself to your peer group or to people you know. It means endeavoring to be the best possible version of yourself in everything you do and not settling for anything less. You see, settling for comfort, mediocrity, and low standards is the easy option. I remember living in housing commission, my family lucky to scrape by week to week. My father told me, "We are doing all right; at least we have food on the table and a roof over our heads" – when, in fact, we were in the lower end of the socioeconomic income bracket. That was just what he used to say to make himself feel better so he didn't have to admit that he had low standards. The question I asked myself for years was: why didn't we have the same income, wealth, and quality of life that my friends did? Why didn't we have the same standards?

I believe that the answer is due to fear. My father, and many like him, feared the pain of rejection, the fear of failure, and not living up to his own expectations and letting his family down. Fear is why a majority of people don't go on to achieve anything of significance in their lives.

As with many of the beliefs you currently hold close, it is important to realize that the foundation of many of your standards may not have come from you; many of them may have been influenced by or come from your parents.

We grow up with our parents' standards, and really, they are all we know – despite the fact that, in this day and age and for your unique and individual life, your parents' standards may not benefit or work for you.

If we aren't on our toes and conscious of the direction that life is taking us, we fall victim to inheriting not only the standards of our parents, but also the standards society dictates; we may go with the flow rather than the standard of living that would produce the quality of life we once imagined.

"Only dead fish go with the flow."
– Andy Hunt

The One-Horse Race

When you consciously set standards for your life, whether it be how you expect to be treated, how you expect to treat others, where you live, the quality of the food you eat, or the quality of relationship you are willing to settle for, you are deciding on what meets and exceeds your highest standards and what does and doesn't meet your lowest standards.

These standards are reflected in the promises you keep, your values, the quality of your work, the fashion of your clothing, your weight, your health and fitness, and your finances. In reality, everything you do reveals the personal standards you live by. By setting your standards and living by them, you attract and notice people with similar expectations instead of constantly having to justify your point of view to people who have differing values.

Don't forget, your life is a one-horse race. The only person you compete against is the best possible version of yourself. Comparing your standards to others' wastes valuable time and energy. Their standards and way of living are not going to allow you to achieve your goals and objectives. All too often, I find people lowering their standards to match those of their peer group so their peers feel better. If you have decided to have higher standards, then you cannot compare yourself to anyone else.

By setting higher standards, you increase the probability of achieving what is possible. You demand more not only from yourself but also from the people around you as well. Because of this, you are prepared to go further, try harder to achieve the outcome you're after – all of which increases your chances of achieving your goals.

The standards you set will depend on the amount of work you're willing to put in and the goals you wish to achieve. These two factors alone will dictate the foundations of the personal standards you live by.

> **"A person who wants to lead the orchestra,**
> **must turn his back on the crowd."**
> **– Max Lucado**

Goal Models

Although I do not recommend comparing yourself with others and their standards, I am a firm believer of "you are who you surround yourself with." By this, I mean you should surround yourself with people who have high standards and whom you aspire to be like. Better known as role models or mentors, these people have high standards in all aspects of their lives. Using them as an inspiration and a benchmark will assist you in helping you raise your own standards. Find role models in every aspect or facet of your life where you're looking for growth and development.

Becoming accountable for your actions is the first ingredient in successfully raising your standards. Regardless of how lofty your aspirations and goals are, accepting low standards will not allow you to reach them. If your standards are not currently where you want them, something has to change . . . and more times than not, that change must be in you.

Is it that easy, though? How do you escape from and improve the standards that are currently keeping you in mediocrity?

Simple:

Decide to make a change.

I have never seen anyone begin a life transformation without first getting fed up with their own lies and excuses. If you truly want higher standards, it all starts with you. You need to acknowledge and admit that you are sick and tired of how your life is and that you need to make a change for the better. Once you can acknowledge this and have taken that first step, you are on your way.

The bottom line is: **the standards you want to achieve are completely within your control**. So take a minute and decide in which areas of your life you need to raise your standards. This will require honesty and for you to be conscious of what you do and how you think every day.

> **"The best day of your life is the one on which you decide your life is your own. No apologies or excuses. No one to lean on, rely on, or blame. The gift is yours – it is an amazing journey – and you alone are responsible for the quality of it.**
>
> **This is the day your life really begins."**
> **– Bob Moawad**

Goals Are Dreams with Deadlines

When speaking to younger soldiers, I talked about them setting goals and having plans for their lives. It's true that most people plan their vacations with better care than they plan their lives. I used three metaphors to explain what goals were and their importance.

1. For the first metaphor, I would ask the soldiers to think of a goal as a ladder. The top of the ladder is your long-term goal. Without the rungs on the ladder, which are short-term goals, you cannot reach the top.

2. For the second metaphor, I would engage with someone in the audience and ask him to imagine that I had just handed him a loaded rifle. I would then point to an undefined large area of the room and ask him to hit the target. I would get louder with my demand to hit the target until eventually the person looked up at me with an expression of bewilderment and confusion and said he didn't know where the target was.

That's exactly the same as in life. If you don't know what you're aiming for and what your goals are, it's difficult to hit the target.

3. For the third metaphor, I compared goals with Google Maps. Not having goals or a clear plan of what you want out of life is like walking to a destination and not knowing how to get there. If you have Google Maps and plotted a route, you eliminate the frustration of going around in circles and wasting time and energy. Life without a plan or goals is no different from wandering around lost.

I'll leave you with one more metaphor:

Have you ever tried to put a jigsaw together without the box top? Depending on the complexity of the puzzle, it can be nearly impossible – and it would take a long time even if you managed it.

Life is pretty much the same.

When we don't have a picture of what we want to achieve in our lives, success becomes a struggle. When we know exactly what we're looking for, most of the time, the pieces just fall into place.

> **"Do not wait: the time will never be 'just right.' Start where you stand, and work with whatever tools you may have at your command, and better tools will be found as you go along."**
> **– Napoleon Hill**

Design Your Goals

The primary reason people don't write down goals or resolutions is because they have a fear of failure. **"What happens if I don't reach that goal?" "What happens if I fail?"** These are the questions and excuses I normally hear. Starting is the hardest part, but once you get started, you develop momentum and things become easier.

For Google Maps to work, you must type in a destination and where you want to go. The site will design the best possible route to get you there, and if you follow the route, you will arrive at your destination.

Goal setting works in a very similar way. By visualizing a clear mental picture of your goal, you can design a vision board and an action plan and prioritize how you are going to get to your destination. Just like the rungs of a ladder, each short-term goal is a small milestone designed to get you closer to your ultimate goal.

Once you have a clear plan and have established what your goals are, everything seems to conspire to move you closer to your goal. Concentrating on what you want will make the how's inevitably appear.

The Breakdown

The human brain is similar to a heat-seeking missile. It seeks out things that are relevant to what you wish to achieve. Once the brain knows what you want, your subconscious mind will go into overdrive to ensure that you achieve your goal.

The more detailed the steps you can break your goals down into, the better. Start with the end in mind, visualize it, picture it, and even try to feel it. Once you are in this state of mind, start asking yourself questions like, **"How can I have this?" "What will it take for me to achieve this?" "What do I need to do to get here?"** Once you start asking yourself these valuable questions, your brain will start providing answers or excuses.

Don't let the excuses stop or deter you. Anything that comes into your mind, write down or record. I'll say it again: the more detailed, the better. Include specific but realistic dates by which you would like to have these goals achieved. Then your subconscious will start to go to work. It will concentrate and fixate on anything associated with what you have decided on.

Along the winding and bumpy road to fulfilling your goals and becoming successful, you are going to encounter obstacles and setbacks. These obstacles vary from not having enough time to not having enough money to the necessity and time needed to learn and develop new skills to friends and family disapproving or not supporting you to fear of failure. If you are not clear with the details of your goals, it is easy to lose focus and to fall victim to these obstacles.

The key to overcoming obstacles is to anticipate them and devise a plan for when they arise so you know how you will deal with them. This is like being one step ahead of someone who is trying to sabotage your dreams.

An obstacle is usually something external and not within your control. These obstacles vary from lack of financial resources to weather conditions to the economy – just to name a few. No one is immune from these hardships and stumbling blocks; they are sent to test you and help you to grow.

If you don't come across obstacles and hardships in the pursuit of achieving your goals, that just means your goal isn't big enough and you are not gaining any self-improvement.

Most see obstacles as a sign to quit or give up, but if achieving your goals were easy, everyone would do it.

By getting through these obstacles, you will change, and with that change will come self-improvement. Any tangible things you acquire can be gone in the blink of an eye if you make poor decisions, but the lessons you learn from the obstacles and the hardships you encounter whilst pursuing your goals are yours forever.

"If it doesn't challenge you, it won't change you."
– Fred Devito

Winners Find a Way. Losers Find an Excuse.

Let's talk more about setting goals and going for what you want. If you are one of those chosen few who know what they want and intend to work for the goals they have set and take action (GOYA), then you have successfully learned the skills you need.

In Chapter 9, you'll learn that your greatest foe is procrastination. If you want to achieve something in life, you cannot linger or wait. Setting goals for every aspect of your life – career, health, family, finances, and relationships – is doable. You know that you should not waste your time hoping for something better when you can do something about it.

> **"I didn't come here to be average."**
> **– Michael Jordan**

Synchronizing Your Goals

When you set a specific goal (after making a conscious decision to get exactly what you want), something happens to your brain. It starts picking up data that you never would have paid attention to before. For instance, if you want to buy a specific car or outfit, you start to notice cars or outfits everywhere.

You start asking yourself if there were always cars and outfits there. Were other people driving and wearing the same thing the whole time? They probably were, but you failed to notice them before because your brain was not paying attention to those things. This is because the brain has a screening function that filters out most of what your senses perceive. If there were no such mechanism, you might have noticed millions of details including the beating of your heart, the sound of traffic outside the window, the wind blowing, and the birds humming outside.

The brain screens out most of our thoughts. Most of what's going on around us is deleted. The part of the brain that knows what we really want makes us notice the things that are relevant to our goals. The reason why you keep seeing cars or outfits is that you have set your mind to acquiring one and thus they have now become important to you.

This part of the brain is called the RAS or Reticular Activating System. The RAS instructs your brain on what it should pay attention to. Once you have set your mind on what you want, the stuff that's related to your wants begins to pop up, and your brain tends to zone in on it. It comes into focus because it has been deemed relevant and significant.

People have different names for this phenomenon. Some call it "synchronicity," while others go for "coincidental." To simplify what's happening, think about it this way. All these things around you (cars, clothes, houses, holidays, etc.) have always been around you. The reason why you never noticed them before is that they were not important to you. They only came into prominence after you set goals wherein you wanted to acquire things – in this case, any of the above.

Get yourself on the right track and start setting your goals today. If you're going to be here and alive, then there is a need, a necessity to make a difference. In fact, you can begin by assigning a responsibility to yourself. Be motivated to make the lives of the people and the groups you encounter much better. Making a difference in the world will make you feel good about yourself – what goes around comes around, so they say. You can make your life count and make it valuable to someone other than yourself. The world can become a better place because of your presence.

When the day ends, cap it with pride and satisfaction since you have accomplished all that you could and have given it 100%. When there are mistakes, put up your hand and take accountability, but do not dwell on them. The sooner you forget, the better your life will be.

Tomorrow is a new day, and you should be so excited about starting it that your spirit and passion to achieve whatever it is you want to do are so strong that no negatives can creep in and trouble or burden you.

> **"It is not in the stars to hold our destiny**
> **but in ourselves."**
> **– William Shakespeare**

Freedom and Options

Life is all about freedom and options. That's why no one wants to go to jail or prison. If you're locked up, your freedoms are taken from you and your options become limited.

People who strive for success and wealth do so because they want to experience more freedom. This is the simple truth behind the race for power and wealth. If you have freedom in life, you can get the most out of it. You'll have the means to do what you enjoy doing the most.

But the real question is, how many of us are free in the real sense?

- Are there many of us who can afford to go on vacation for six months? Can we not worry about losing our jobs? How many of us can decide to leave a career and begin with an entry-level job in another field?

- How many of us can just pack up our belongings and move to another city or perhaps a foreign country?

The more success we attain, the more money we have to do these things. Our options become endless.

Most of us cannot afford to do any of these things. If you think about it, we aren't free at all. The truth is that we are the ones who have put the shackles on our own hands and feet. We have impeded our capability to make the most out of life. In fact, we are the ones who have set limitations on our opportunities for freedom and growth.

We fail at being truly happy because we allow societal expectations and peer pressure to dictate what we think are the most important things in our lives. We pursue goals set for us by society, and we keep wondering why we do not feel as happy as we thought we'd be when we fulfill them. In our rush to keep up with the Joneses, we don't stop and realize that the Joneses aren't that happy. The reason the grass is greener on the other side of the fence is because the person on the other side takes the time and effort to water the garden and maintain it.

> **"I'm too busy working on my own grass to notice if yours is greener."**
> **– Unknown**

For far too many people, life is nothing but a competition to succeed and live a luxurious life. And in all their efforts to live this opulent lifestyle, they are not actually living at all.

Ever heard of the theory of survival of the fittest? Today, it's survival of the richest. If you haven't done well in life, if you aren't successful, your life is considered a failure. You spend your life living the dreams of others, making them happy while trying to make a way for yourself in this fast-paced world.

When is the time to smile a little?

Even a social gathering is now a competition. Who has a better car? Who has a better dress? How expensive was his watch? It is a shallow age we are living in.

We switch jobs, change careers, run after the best opportunities, fall in and out of love, and, in this dynamic lifestyle, we forget to embrace the beauty of this life given to us. Poet W.H. Davies correctly wrote, "What is this life if, full of care/ We have no time to stand and stare?"

You are the product of millions of years of evolution. Your body is more intricate than any NASA space project. Your mind is more powerful and faster than any computer known to mankind – it's like owning a Ferrari, Lamborghini, or Bugatti, only better – and it is controlled without you being conscious of it. Why take life so seriously? No one gets out alive, so you may as well enjoy it.

Today, almost everyone slogs their way through work and buys a house or a car to live a standard, mediocre life. But very few people really live.

> **"It takes courage to do what you want.**
> **Other people have a lot of plans for you."**
> **– Joseph Campbell**

My Takeaway for this chapter:

Pick an area in your life you wish to change. Start by trying to improve your standards in one aspect of your life at a time.

Ask yourself whether you surround yourself with the right people to improve that area of your life.

Only you can raise your standards. Doing so starts with first making a choice and identifying that things need to change.

The biggest gamble you will make is not doing what you want and thinking you can buy yourself the freedom to do it later on in life.

Chapter 8: Believe You Can, and You're Halfway There

"Confidence is: going after Moby Dick in a row
boat and taking the tartar sauce with you."
–Zig Ziglar

Believe and Achieve

In order for you to be successful, the first and probably the most important ingredient is believing that you are capable of making your goal happen. This quiet self-confidence and self-belief are fundamental to your success. The belief that you can achieve a goal starts with a choice and a conscious decision. That choice develops into a habit, and that habit ultimately becomes a mindset that you develop over time.

Most of us come from some type of dysfunctional family, some worse than others. We inherit our parents' beliefs, but the past is the past, and nothing is achieved by blaming someone else for your level of self-confidence. It's up to you to take charge of and change your beliefs.

**"You are not responsible for the programming
you picked up in childhood.**

**However, as an adult, you are one hundred
percent responsible for fixing it."**
– Ken Keyes, Jr.

Remember, the Ark was Built by Amateurs; the Titanic by Professionals.

If you invest your time in positive affirmations, positive visualization, and self-education, you can learn to do almost anything. Successful people will tell you that they were not the most skillful or talented in their field, but they chose to believe that they could achieve whatever they put their minds to. It all starts with the belief.

I am a good example of believing in yourself. I had my first boxing match as a bantamweight (54kg or 118lbs) and was over 6 feet tall. I was always a skinny kid – the skinny kid who was always too small or too scrawny to be any good at anything. I used to listen to what people would say, but instead of discouraging me, their words motivated me – because I knew I had something that most other people didn't have: I would always go the extra mile. I would make the biggest effort, and I would be the most determined. They were the three things I had going for me: **effort**, **belief**, and **determination**.

Why is making an effort so difficult for some people to achieve? Probably because a) the thought of having to make more of an effort casts doubt on their ability, and b) most importantly, if they make an effort, they are left without any excuses for failure.

Without making an effort, you can always say "I could have been anything." However, once you try and have made an effort, you cannot say that anymore and your excuses are taken from you.

I once had a soldier approach me and say that he could have made it into Special Forces. If he had really tried for it, he wouldn't have been able to say that.

I knew I had to overcome people's opinions and judgments or I would never achieve anything. If I had believed the naysayers and cynics who said I couldn't do something, I wouldn't have accomplished much.

> **"The problem with close-minded people is
> they always have their mouths open."**
> **– Zig Ziglar**

While in the army, I made a conscious decision to not worry about what other people thought of me. That was one of the greatest decisions of my life, and I am grateful that I had the guts to follow it through.

At the end of the day, you don't need to justify your decisions or beliefs to anyone. The opinions and judgments of other people just don't matter. Trust your own intuition and gut instinct. What's the worst that could happen? You could fall on your backside! If that happens, dust yourself off and try again. Just try to learn from it and avoid making the same mistake twice. Most people waste so much time being fearful of what others think and trying to compete with their peers! Who cares what they have, what they think? Your life is a one-horse race, and you are competing against no one else but yourself. Save yourself time and anxiety and concentrate on your own goals.

**"When you're 18,
you worry about what everybody is thinking of you;**

**when you're 40,
you don't give a darn what anybody thinks of you;**

**when you're 60,
you realize nobody's been thinking about you at all."
– Dr. Daniel Amen**

The Most Important Thing You Can Wear Is Your Confidence

Every successful person has a great deal of confidence or faith in his/her ability to achieve the goal at hand. Having confidence doesn't mean you present yourself as being cocky, but rather that you express yourself with a great deal of assuredness and confidence.

Having self-confidence is not only a positive feature and quality to have in life; it also enables us to not be susceptible to our fears and doubts and to be certain in our decision making. Most people have a fear of failure and rejection, and at times this can affect their self-confidence. These are natural human emotions that are sometimes tough habits to break. The trick is to act in spite of them, which is something we all get better at over time.

You can always tell who people with high levels of self-confidence are, as they have an infectious aura of positivity and optimism that is easy to be around. They inspire others to be better, which is why people are drawn to them. Confidence is believing in your ability and knowing you have the talent to back it. It is understanding and accepting your strengths and weaknesses in any situation.

> **"Self-confidence is the most attractive quality**
> **a person can have. How can anyone see how**
> **great you are if you can't see it yourself?"**
> **– Unknown**

Confidence is a Cycle

Having self-confidence allows you to give people confidence, and those people will give it back to you – boosting your sense of self-worth and creating a sustainable loop of positive social energy.

Confidence is not about being bigger than anyone else or about the inability to fail. True confidence is an open-mindedness that encourages different opinions and perceptions.

On the flip side of the coin is overconfidence – an undesirable personality trait that borders on arrogance.

Overconfidence is bragging or boasting without having the skills or know-how to back it up. The difference can be easily identified and is felt in a change of social energy.

Being a know-it-all incapable of accepting influence from others can make you unbearable to be around. A truly self-confident person is willing to be proven wrong and is able to show honesty and acknowledge prior mistakes.

Both confident and overconfident people are aware of personal areas of strength and ability. However, the difference lies in the fact that while a person with self-confidence has no trouble appreciating others' abilities and strengths, an overconfident person cannot. Furthermore, confident people have no need for the admiration of others to make them feel secure. They show their abilities through their actions, not by their words. Having self-confidence means realizing your ability; being overconfident means boasting and letting others know all about your ability.

Being overconfident is closely related to arrogance. Through this arrogance, overconfident people build themselves up by putting others down. Arrogance achieves its energy from stealing the confidence and self-respect of others. Arrogant people judge their own self-worth by comparing themselves with others, bluff their way to success, and find it difficult to listen if the conversation is not centered on them. They tend to avoid risk and are quick to lay blame if things do not work out as planned or the way they expected. Most over-confident and arrogant people are bullies and subconsciously feel inferior – hence why they are normally so mouthy.

Long-term self-confidence is a logical assessment of your abilities rather than a charged-up emotional feeling. You just know you have a certain value. You raise that by having real accomplishments and strengths and by getting enough feedback from the outside world that you know you're on the right track.

"Be so busy improving yourself that you have
no time to criticize others."
– Chetan Bhagat

My Takeaway for this chapter:

How to be more confident.

Stop comparing yourself to others, and focus on improving yourself in every aspect of your life.

Set small goals. Break a goal into steps, and you are more likely to succeed. Small successes fuel big changes in your self-confidence.

Be optimistic and look for the positives in every situation.

Love yourself. Yes, I said it. If you're not being treated with the love and respect you deserve, check your mental price tag. Perhaps you have marked yourself down or, worse still, let other people mark you down. Value yourself more.

Let things wash over you. Don't sweat the small stuff.

Chapter 9: Continuing in Spite of Fear

"Fear is an idea-crippling, experience-
crushing, success-stalling inhibitor
inflicted only by yourself."
– Stephanie Melish

Just Keep Going

Pardon the pun, but mental fitness is a state of mind. When people find themselves in difficult situations, some of them give up, some of them do nothing but complain, and some of them keep driving themselves forward. Once you're in the mental state of driving yourself forward, large quantities of energy are expended to fuel thoughts and to take your mind off pain and discomfort.

People who can achieve the mindset of not giving up and having good, old-fashioned perseverance are normally the top achievers in life. No matter how hard the struggle gets, these people never take the easier option; they just keep going.

What Keeps You Going?

Is it a passion for not losing or giving up?

Is it a particular motivation?

Perseverance?

Stubbornness?

The key to developing success in a competitive arena, whether it be in work or in personal life, is the ability to be mentally disciplined, to have the necessary mental toughness to block out distractions. Mental toughness means thinking in the correct frame of mind, and it takes discipline and the ability to recognize when your emotional level is higher than your ability to focus and relax.

Let's talk about an example here: an athlete. The basic principle is that the athlete must think positively at all times. The objective is to focus on the positive and banish negative thoughts from your mind. To be strong physically as well as mentally doesn't occur as a matter of good fortune. You must train your mind in certain ways, most of which can be done subconsciously. Control of your body and its feelings and thoughts is critical. A few techniques to increase your mental discipline are as follows:

1. When feeling anxious or nervous, slow down your breathing, take deep breaths, and exhale slowly.

2. Focus your eyes on one thing and then slowly and deliberately move to another.

3. Consciously relax, tighten, and release any body parts that feel tense.

4. Continually reinforce positive thoughts, even when you are afraid or doubtful.

Fear Is a Liar

Now, what keeps you from continuing?

Fear?

Most forms of fear are illusions we create in our own minds. Fear is almost always about what is going to happen next – meaning you are afraid of something that does not currently exist.

If the thing you fear does not exist, then it is purely imagined. Suffering from a fear of things that are non-existent is one definition of insanity. As such, there's a huge community of people in the world today with a level of insanity that is socially accepted.

People tend to worry about things that either happened in the past or can happen in the future – a form of suffering that is due to something that currently doesn't exist. Don't get me wrong here: danger is real. But fear is a choice that we actually decide upon which is one part memory and one part imagination. Being lost in your imagination and allowing your mind to wander is the origin of your fear.

But if you live in the now, you will feel no fear.

Fear limits your vision and fuels low self-esteem. Fear can be used as an excuse that stops you from seeing and reaching your true potential, and the low self-esteem it generates keeps you enslaved in things that you are reluctant to do.

It is scientifically proven that we are all born with two innate fears: the fear of falling and the fear of loud noises. These are built into our DNA, and we are born with them primarily as survival mechanisms.

So where did all those other fears that you have come from?

Well, you were not born with them, so no doubt you have experienced something undesirable (either consciously or subconsciously) while you were growing up, and you now associate that pain or danger with whatever it is that you fear. These experiences, which you perceive will cause you harm, are what you try to avoid so you don't feel those same emotions again.

To put it another way: you have learned your fear.

So how do you overcome your fear? How do you keep it from consuming and paralyzing you, from hindering your daily progress towards achieving your goals?

Simple.

Be motivated by your fear.

This is a mindset shift that will take work, but it is well worth the effort.

What do I mean by that?

Anytime you have a fear, attack it. Don't be scared of it.

The best way to conquer fear is to repeatedly force yourself to face whatever it is you're afraid of. Constant exposure to what you perceive you're afraid of will help to condition you and your mind until the fear diminishes. Anxiety and fear become less powerful the more you face and deal with them.

> **"You will never do anything in this world**
> **without courage."**
> **– Aristotle**

My Biggest Fear

Everyone is different, and out of the seven billion people on this planet, not one single person is on the same journey as another. That is why it is important for us to try not to judge people; other people are on a different path from us, and we have never walked a mile in their shoes. Just because they are on a different path does not mean they are on the wrong path; it just means that their path is different to ours.

In saying that, let me share something with you – my biggest fear.

As an average person brought up in Western culture, you are constantly bombarded with expectations –

expectations to study and do well at school so you can ultimately do well in life. You feel pressured to survive and succeed.

When you leave school, you get a job, switch jobs over the years, grab opportunities here and there, and work really hard to succeed. Then you get married, work even harder, and make more money. Sometime between the ages of 30-40, you have attained pretty much everything anyone could hope for. You have done your parents proud and are a good husband or wife and parent as well.

Three or four decades fly by. You have worked hard and taken care of your family. Before you know it, you are 80 and lying on a hospital bed, knowing you have just a few hours left. You close your eyes, and your whole life flashes before you. It's only then, in your final moments, that you realize that in your race to attain success, you have forgotten to live.

You were so caught up in fulfilling the dreams of your parents and family that you never considered what your own dreams might be. You suddenly hope for just a few more days, weeks, even months to live a little, to see the world, to smile.

And that's how you die: without living.

You live the most precious years of your life struggling and chasing after money, love, relationships, and success.

This story defines my biggest fear – to die without really living.

That is why you need a break. A break to value your life, a break to value yourself!

Realize your needs and dreams, and take the time to smile and do what makes you happy. You don't want to reach 80 and find that you have no time left to do what really matters to you.

So wherever you are in life, remember that success is not everything. Take a minute, close your eyes, embrace your dreams, and live them. Get out of your claustrophobic workplace and have fun.

When was the last time you did anything fun?

Youth and spontaneity go hand in hand. When we are younger, we don't give a second thought to being impulsive and very rarely think of **"Will this work?"** or **"Will I land on my feet?"**

Now that you're older, when was the last time you've done something completely spontaneous? Something that wasn't planned, that didn't fit into your five-year plan, that took you outside of your comfort zone?

Life's too short. Live it . . . and live it now!

Ready or not, someday it will all come to an end.

There will be no more sunrises, no minutes, hours, or days.

All things you collected, whether treasured or forgotten, will pass to someone else.

Your wealth, fame, and temporal power will shrivel to irrelevance.

Your grudges, resentments, frustrations, and jealousies will finally disappear.

So too your hopes, ambitions, plans, and to-do lists will expire.

The wins and losses that once seemed so important will fade away.

It won't matter where you came from, or on what side of the tracks you lived, at the end.

It won't matter whether you were beautiful or brilliant.

Even your gender and skin color will be irrelevant.

So what will matter? How will the value of your days be measured?

What will matter is not what you bought, but what you built;

Not what you got, but how you gave.

What will matter is not your success, but your significance.

What will matter is not what you learned, but what you taught.

What will matter is every act of integrity, compassion, courage, or sacrifice that enriched, empowered, or encouraged others to emulate your example.

What will matter is not your competence, but your character.

What will matter is not how many people you knew, but how many will feel a lasting loss when you're gone.

What will matter are not your memories, but the memories that live in those who loved you.

What will matter is how long you will be remembered, by whom, and for what.

Living a life that matters doesn't happen by accident.

It's not a matter of circumstance, but of choice.

Choose to live a life that matters.

© Michael Josephson 2003
www.whatwillmatter.org
Reprinted with permission.

Procrastination Is Not Laziness but Fear

Almost every one of us procrastinates at one time or another. Researchers in the US recently discovered that 80-95% of university students procrastinate on a regular basis on assignments or projects. In this technological age, phones, tablets, computers, and games give people a continual starting point for putting things off, but technology is not fully to blame. Individuals who procrastinate normally have spontaneous or impulsive personalities and value what they can have today more than what they can have tomorrow. The human brain has a way of exaggerating how big an impending task or project may be. It also has a tendency to concentrate only on the most difficult parts, which is where procrastination starts. When the brain only focuses on the enormity and more difficult points of a project, it starts to find ways to avoid work and fools us into thinking we're busier than we actually are.

As human beings, we look for things that have immediate gratification or outcomes. Checking emails and Facebook is easier right now than finishing a job you perceive will take a lot longer and require more effort. We must understand that procrastination is not laziness but more so fear. Dreading or fearing something makes us want to deter or postpone even thinking about it and to do something easy and immediate instead to fulfill our instant gratification urges. Not having negative consequences now doesn't mean there won't be ramifications later.

> **"Procrastination is like a credit card:**
> **it's a lot of fun until you get the bill."**
> **– Christopher Parker**

The Two Types of Procrastinators

Even if these fears are on a subconscious level, they hinder us and keep us from achieving our immediate goals. This continues until we start to a) become anxious and concerned about the result, which leads to b) us being forced to either get the job done or give up. The goal is to confront your biggest problem by tackling the most difficult and demanding projects first thing each day and endeavoring to develop momentum. Once you start something, regardless of the size, your brain will be tempted to finish it or see it through to some type of perceived conclusion. Once you get into this state of mind and gain momentum, you start to see that the project's not as big a mountain as you made it out to be, and that the work involved isn't so daunting after all.

There are many types of procrastination, but fear and assumptions are at the root of every single one.

The one I relate to the most is the perfectionist – the person who gets a project started but becomes too consumed with the details and making everything perfect. Perfectionists tend to procrastinate because they have such high standards and expectations – which lead to anxiety over whether or not they can meet those standards.

Another trait of perfectionists who procrastinate is that they look at an incomplete project and feel that they are not getting anywhere, rather than recognizing each small accomplishment that moves them closer to a finished product.

Another example is of a person who lives in the future. A bucket list is a prime example of what I am talking about. We have a list of things we would like to do and achieve, and because we have time on our side, we believe that although life is too busy now, we will get to our list down the track. The reality is that the future will not be that much different, and our future self won't be tremendously productive and focused either; our future self is also lazy and inefficient and will no doubt have too much on its plate down the track as well.

Not only can procrastination have a negative impact on your productivity and the achievement of your goals, but it can also have an impact on your relationships. By procrastinating and putting things off, you place a strain on the people around you. If things arc left to the last minute or don't get done, the people who depend on you – whether they be co-workers, friends, family, or even teammates – can over time become resentful. Regardless of the size of the job and how daunting it looks, try to break it down into smaller, more manageable chunks. Dissect the project into several steps and create a list detailing the process you need to take in order for you to accomplish each task.

A simple change of your perceptions and a positive mindset can also help with procrastination. Enjoying what you do and being excited by the challenge that it presents focuses you on the positives and gives you a feeling of satisfaction when the job is achieved.

When you succeed, take time to savor the moment so you will remember how good it feels. This will get you in the right mindset when faced with another huge task.

Fear of Failure

I was speaking with a friend of mine who has spent decades climbing the corporate ladder and becoming a success in his chosen field.

The conversation moved toward being successful and how fear can be used as a motivator to succeed if channeled correctly. He mentioned that he'd lived most of his life in fear: fear of being fired, fear of having nothing. Although I found it difficult to understand why a man of his stature and standing within the community felt like this, this indicated to me that his primary fear was a fear of failure and of losing what he had worked so hard his whole life to achieve. This made me realize that the meaning of failure and how we perceive it has changed from being an acknowledgement ("I failed") to a character flaw ("I am a failure").

"The greatest barrier to success is the fear of failure."
– Sven Goran Eriksson

Although every human being is born with the two innate fears as I mentioned previously, the fear of failure is not only very real but extremely common. A constant and persistent fear of failure is a form of phobia known as **atychiphobia**. People can build up this fear so strongly in their mind that they never attempt to achieve anything at all. This doesn't mean they don't have hopes and dreams like the rest of us, but it does mean they will never try to attain them. Having that confined mindset causes you to never realize that you have already failed, simply by not trying. You let your imagination run wild, and you dream of the perfect life – but at the same time, you are aware that you will never have the life you want because you know that you are the one holding yourself back.

The Root of Atychiphobia

To get to the root of the problem, we must first understand what fear of failure actually means.

Any phobia or fear stems from the unconscious. One person's definition of failure may be different from the next person's due to varying personal standards, values, and belief systems. How a person perceives something will determine whether he or she considers that thing a learning experience or the end of the world. That's why controlling your state of mind and perceptions should always be at the top of your to-do list and something that you are working on constantly.

Are you conscious of how you act in response to failure? Do you perceive failure as a lesson or a catastrophe?

If you fail and start to convince yourself that you are incapable of something and you believe it, you will begin to feel inadequate and will stop trying – worst still, will not try at all. That is why so many people never achieve their full potential. At some time in their life, they failed at something and convinced themselves that they were, are, and will be a failure – and that belief became embedded. Once you believe and are certain of something, it becomes extremely difficult to change your mind.

We have been brought up to believe that failure is negative and that we should do whatever it takes to avoid it. Most people are not willing to give failure a second opportunity. Landing on their backsides once was a bad enough experience and more than most can handle. We constantly define ourselves by the mistakes and failures of our past. Those failures are not who you are now or the person you have grown to be. You are better every single day as a result of learning from those failures.

If you're willing to learn from your failures and perceive defeat as a blessing or lesson in disguise rather than a negative, then you are well and truly on the road to success.

Failure is 100% dependent on how we look at it.

Failures, mistakes, and blunders will only stop you if you let them. Some of the greatest minds and personalities in history who have inspired me and the world have experienced failure, and on more than one occasion.

> **"Success is the ability to go from one failure to another with no loss of enthusiasm."**
> **– Sir Winston Churchill**

Famous Failures

Bill Gates, the richest man in the world at the time of writing this book, not only dropped out of college and was unable to get his degree, but he also failed miserably in his first business venture. This self-made billionaire is a testament to the fact that failure is not a bad thing as long as you learn from it.

Oprah Winfrey failed and was fired from her first television job as a news anchor and told she wasn't fit for television. Oprah believes that "There is no such thing as failure – it is just life moving us in another direction."

Vincent Van Gogh is considered one of the greatest artists of all time, yet, prior to his death, he'd only sold one painting. During his lifetime, critics declared him a failure. But over 100 years after his passing, our contemporary appreciation of his paintings is testimony to the creative brilliance he possessed and the appreciation and recognition he was deprived of when he was alive.

Probably one of my favorite failure stories is that of Elvis Presley. Elvis was one of the greatest entertainers in the history of music. He got knocked to the ground and told he was no good on more than one occasion. Elvis failed an audition for a local vocal quartet, the Songfellows, and was told that he did not demonstrate an ear for harmony. After this setback, he returned to being a truck driver. It wasn't until a friend suggested he contact Eddie Bond, who had an opening for a vocalist in his band, that he gave music another try. Elvis was again rejected, this time by Eddie Bond, who advised Elvis to stick to truck driving "because you're never going to make it as a singer." Elvis persisted and didn't let failure or setbacks get the better of him. The rest, as they say, is history.

Failure as a Teacher

We all stumble and fall, make mistakes and poor decisions. No one is immune from that. But imagine if Bill Gates had given up on his dream to develop Microsoft after his first business failure. Imagine if Oprah Winfrey had listened to her detractors, who told her that she was no good and should find another career.

Think how differently your life would be if you'd let your failures stop you.

Failure can be the best of teachers. Without failure, we would never realize how strong we are, would never be forced to find the extra motivation to succeed. A deep knowledge of yourself and finding out who your truest friends are can only surface from failure. The key to success is understanding and learning from these valuable life lessons. We should recognize and acknowledge that we can fail. Facing that thought and accepting it is not only courageous; it is the best attitude to achieving a successful and more enjoyable life.

Most people have a fear of failure due to the fear of the unknown. Maintaining a positive mindset and having the knowledge that you will land on your feet is an effective way to build self-confidence. A great way of improving your self-confidence and reducing your fear of failure is by setting and visualizing short-term goals. I am talking about small goals that will give you a few small wins that will, in turn, boost your confidence and give you the conviction to look for bigger and more challenging goals.

> "I'd rather attempt to do something great and fail than to attempt to do nothing and succeed."
> – Robert H. Schuller

My Takeaway for this chapter:

Try not to exaggerate and blow things out of proportion. This is where excuses will start to develop, and you won't be realistic about getting the job done. Try and also change your mindset to "I get to" rather than "I have to."

Imagine being on your deathbed and fading in and out of consciousness. Due to high levels of medication, you start to dream and hallucinate. It's like your life is flashing before your eyes. You see a lifetime of hopes, dreams, ideas, abilities, and talents that you once possessed, but which, for whatever reason, you never went after. You never went after those dreams, you never acted on those ideas, and you never used those talents – all because you were afraid to fail.

Don't be afraid to fail. Be afraid of not trying.

Chapter 10: 'You Learn From Your Mistakes'.

A Wise Person Learns From His Own Mistakes.
A Genius Learns From Others' Mistakes and
Then Does Something About It.
- Unkown

In Every Mistake, There is Potential for Growth.

The ability to learn and grow based on what others have gone through is one I hold close. While we can't change our past, we can change our present and future. How our life pans out from here is dependent on what we do starting today. Death comes to all of us at some point. Having the insights of people who have lived to the end of their life is strikingly helpful in living our best life. Speaking with others who have lived a full and long life can help you understand the lessons they learned before it becomes too late to put those lessons into practice.

Nothing behind us can change, but every moment from now till the end is completely in our power.

After seeing both of my parents die over a fairly short period of time – and especially after witnessing my mother face her mortality – I began to see my own mortality. I noticed that, before she died, my mother spent a great deal of time in self-reflection on her past – how she lived her life, the time and effort she dedicated to her children, the things she could have changed but didn't.

It took me getting a tumor diagnosis at the age of 40 for me to wake up to the fact that I was not going to be here forever.

The sudden recognition of my own mortality made me realize that the adage of "It's never too late" was false. There will come a point in your life when you are unable to start or complete all your goals or fulfill all your dreams. I realized that goals and dreams come about because of choices we make. While you still have strength and health, honor your dreams and make the choice to realize them.

People at the end of their life often regret missing their child's development or their loved ones' company. What can you do to make sure you do not have the same regrets? Simplify your life and focus on family, friends, and self rather than stuff. Create open space and time to enjoy what you have. If you take anything away from this book, let it be the understanding that life is all about balance.

Some seek to maintain positive relationships with people by pretending to be happy. Not only do they limit themselves and their potential, but they can also become ill due to excess stress and resentment. Honest revelation of your thoughts, dreams, and feelings can lead to more fulfilling relationships and can help you rid yourself of toxic ones.

> **"We all get the same 24 hours – what you do with them reveals where your priorities and values lie."**
> **– Ritchie Gibson**

No One Lacks Potential. You Can Lack Will and Skill, but Everyone Has Potential

Anything is possible; we hear that all the time. What we don't hear is that to make something possible, first you must act. Next time you drive past a cemetery, stop for a moment and think of all the people who have passed, who at one time or another had the potential to become great, but who never acted. Only a small percentage of the people in our world can confess to having achieved all they are capable of.

The majority of people reading this book will be doing relatively well in life. After all, being able to read puts you ahead of the 770 million people who cannot; therefore, I believe you would have a decent standard of education. No doubt you are well fed and have at least a few dollars in your pocket. But despite all that we have going for us and all we are grateful for, most of us still have a frustrating feeling that we could have done more with our lives.

We focus a large part of our lives on living up to the expectations of our parents and peer groups, and often lay blame outside ourselves that we are not as well off or that others have it better than we do. Certain skills and talents have gone undeveloped, and your full potential has never been reached.

If you are agreeing with what I am saying, what is preventing you from fulfilling your potential right now? Are you heading for that graveyard with potential that will never be realized?

Below are a few ingredients I think may be lacking if you perceive you're not fulfilling your potential.

> **"Passion is born when you realize your true potential."**
> **– Ritchie Gibson**

6 Ingredients for Success

Ingredient #1: Backbone and Guts

Method: The first things that you will require in your recipe to fulfill your potential are a backbone and guts. You must be willing to make a change and not listen to any excuses. Everything you require to fulfill your potential is inside you right now.

> **"Stop wearing your wishbone where your**
> **backbone ought to be."**
> **– Elizabeth Gilbert**

Ingredient #2: Self-belief

Method: There is not one other person on this planet who is the same as you. You are an original, one of a kind. There is no improved version of you, no one with the same life experiences, and no one with your enthusiasm for what you wish to achieve. That means that you compete with no one but yourself. If you don't believe in yourself and that you can accomplish great things, neither will anybody else.

Ingredient #3: Action

Method: Action always beats intention. Goal setting and planning are the building blocks to reaching your true potential; however, it is action that leads to success. You can achieve success without skill or talent, but you can never become successful at anything unless you first decide to take action.

Ingredient #4: Time

Method: Time is our most valuable asset. Do you read and educate yourself or watch more TV? It amazes me when people complain that they are not getting anywhere in life or not getting ahead. Could it be because they have made the choice not to educate themselves and instead watch TV, which will not necessarily allow them to grow? This is a choice they made, but they still complain about not being where they want to be in life and fulfilling their potential. If you want to reach your true potential, invest your time wisely.

Ingredient #5: Laziness

Method: Being too lazy and not wanting to put in the work or effort needed is probably a contributing factor to why you're not achieving your true potential.

Ingredient #6: Listen

Method: We are taught from a young age to focus on outcomes rather than the process. It is important to pay attention to what gives you energy and fascinates you. By listening and focusing your energy inside, you may realize that your potential for change is in the present and in you, rather than something in the future that you need to achieve.

You may not understand what your full potential is at the moment. Fulfilling your potential is not a single accomplishment or achievement; it is about a) realizing your vision and b) the person you become during your journey. It is not about an ultimate destination.

> **"Difficulties in your life don't come to destroy you, but to help you realize your hidden potential."**
> **– Unknown**

My Takeaway for this chapter:

One important question that I would like you to think about and ponder.

How do you want to be remembered?

Obviously, there is no right or wrong answer, but this one question pushes you to see yourself as a different person—the person you can become.

It places a mirror before you where, for a brief second, you have to confront whether you can actually live up to your stated values.

I want to be remembered by inspiring others to follow my example. What about you?

Chapter 11: Finding Your Rock Bottom

"Keep away from people who try to belittle your ambitions. Small people always do that, but the really great ones make you feel that you, too, can become great."
– Mark Twain

GOYA

How do you acquire the extreme drive and dedication to be the best you can be? There is no simple answer to this, no detailed step-by-step guide. You first have to have a goal or a vision. Then you have to muster up the necessary energy to get your backside off the lounge and into action.

Remember our motto? GOYA (Get Off Your Ass!)

For the majority of people, the initial motivation comes from hitting their version of rock bottom. Maybe you can't play with your kids anymore because you are too winded after two minutes of a game of tag, or your favorite pair of jeans doesn't make it past your hips. Perhaps you put in an extra 16 hours of work this weekend and realize that you missed your son's big football game or your daughter's dance recital, or, even worse, forgot it was your wedding anniversary.

Take that initial frustration, disgust, or negativity and turn it into positive energy to get yourself restarted. Rather than falling into depression, do something about it!

Write down a plan of action that coincides with your goals, and continue to do so day by day, week by week, and month by month. Apply that energy to propel your mind, soul, and body into action and into achieving your goals.

Don't allow negativity or excuses to set up mental or physical roadblocks. Motivated people understand the importance of visualization and the power of positive thinking.

Focus on your strengths, and let them overcome your weaknesses. Start every day thinking about what you can and will do, and you will mentally set the stage for the rest of the day. Do this every day, and positive thinking will become a habit.

Visual Imagery and Anxiety

Imagery and visualization are key ingredients for success. Visualization means thinking about and seeing yourself perform positively and successfully in all situations, whether they are in training, competition, or just everyday life. Anxiety causes you to speed up your behavior. When you feel tense and anxious, make an effort to slow down your behavior.

Anxiety increases when a person's self-talk is negative and self-defeating. A person who speaks negatively tends to say things like: "Why am I doing this?" or "I can't do it" or "I can't make it." On a side note, remember: when making decisions, there is no such word as "can't"! You either won't or you don't want to. When facing tough decisions or actions, always remember to maintain positive self-talk. Don't give up and take the easy way out.

The worst thing a person can live with is regret. If you know that you couldn't have gone any farther or tried any harder and are convinced that you have given your all, you will have no regrets or negative thoughts.

One of my favorite works of poetry of is called "Don't Quit." It is written by an unknown author, and I've yet to meet a person whose life it didn't apply to at some point.

When things go wrong, as they sometimes will,

When the road you're trudging seems all uphill,

When funds are low and the debts are high,

And you want to smile but you have to sigh,

When care is pressing you down a bit,
Rest if you must, but don't you quit.

Life is queer with its twists and turns,
As every one of us sometimes learns,
And many a failure turns about,
When he might have won if he'd stuck it out.
Don't give up, though the pace seems slow –
You may succeed with another blow.

Often the goal is nearer than
It seems to a faint and faltering man;
Often the struggler has given up
When he might have captured the victor's cup,
And he learned too late, when the night
slipped down,
How close he was to the golden crown.

Success is failure turned inside out –
The silver tint of the clouds of doubt,
And you never can tell how close you are –
It may be near when it seems afar;
So stick to the fight when you're hardest hit –
It's when things seem worst that you mustn't quit.
– Unknown

Can't Is the Real C Word

Can and can't.

Just one letter (and an apostrophe) marks the difference between these words; however, their meanings and how you use them can be the difference between a successful life and an unfulfilled one.

How you see yourself and **the understanding of what you are truly capable of as a human being** are two of the most important things in life.

Unfortunately, the word "can't" is alive and well. It is heard quite a lot these days, but what we don't realize is that it's crippling our lives. When you say "can't," you are victimizing yourself and rendering yourself incompetent and unable to make alterations or improvements to your life.

In reality, when you use the word "can't," you are using it as a defense mechanism to keep yourself emotionally safe. So if you say "I can't pass this exam" or "I can't submit this project by the deadline," it only means that it is your choice not to work hard enough to finish your project on time or to pass your exam. In other words, you have chosen to fail. You think that saying the word "can't" is the easy way out.

> **"Impossible is just a big word thrown around by small men who find it easier to live in the world they've been given than to explore the power they have to change it. Impossible is not a fact. It's an opinion. Impossible is not a declaration. It's a dare. Impossible is potential. Impossible is temporary. Impossible is nothing."**
> **– Muhammad Ali**

Is It Really Impossible?

When you "can't" do something, you imply that doing the thing is not in your control and that there are external factors getting in your way. It's an excuse for your lack of success, and almost everybody hates having their excuses taken away.

Another reason we use the word "can't" is to pretend we have a restriction so we don't have to tell someone the truth. "Can't" gives us the chance to lie. For instance, if you say "I can't make it to the conference," you want to portray that you don't have an option. But the truth is that you don't want to go to the conference. In other words, you are lying to yourself. Trust me, it is not the best feeling. So be honest and tell the truth: you'd rather not go.

When you use the word "can't," you have to do some soul searching and determine if you are being honest or just disguising the truth.

Individuals who take responsibility for their own actions will hardly ever use the word "can't." If you wish to succeed professionally and attain all your goals, the best remedy would be to stop using the word "can't." Remove it from your dictionary and replace it with "I don't want to" or "I choose not to." In this way, you take responsibility for what you do and you don't let outside forces control your decisions.

In a nutshell, if you really "can't" do something, it's because you lack the skill, but if you "won't" do something, it's because you lack the will.

"Whether you think you can, or you think you can't – you're right."
– Henry Ford

Be Impractical. Let People Doubt You. Be Unrealistic.

When people tell you to get real and to stop dreaming, think of those people and feel sorry for them. My mum used to tell me that some people should be pitied, not punished. Some people are just so unhappy with their lives that they will try and burst your bubble of good ideas the first chance they get. She used to say that true courage is the ability of a person to lay a firm foundation with the bricks that others throw at him.

Be impractical. Let people doubt you. Be unrealistic.

It is unrealistic to be in a metal box that weighs 143,000 tons in the middle of the ocean and think that it's going to float. Luckily, Egyptian pharaoh Sneferu[5] thought differently. Many other people have learned from his initial concept, and now we have luxury cruise ships that were once thought unrealistic.

The Wright brothers' own father ridiculed the idea of his sons inventing the first ever flying machine, saying that they should leave flying to the birds. Today, we are able to fly to all corners of the globe because the brothers persevered.

It was once unrealistic to think of an invention such as a mobile phone. Systems for transmitting information between people have been around for centuries, but they only became wireless recently. Wireless telegraphy, which later evolved into radio, was invented by Guglielmo Marconi in 1880. Lucky he didn't think that it was unrealistic and that he decided to persist! By 2020,

---

5   Sneferu: the first king of the 4th dynasty, 2613–2589 BC

approximately 90% of the world's population will have mobile or cell phones.[6]

> **"The greatest pleasure in life is doing what people say you cannot do."**
> **– Walter Bagehot**

Reverse Psychology

I am sure when I was younger, my father tried reverse psychology to motivate me – that is, he told me not to even try because I would only feel let down when I didn't achieve what I set out to do.

I've never accepted that I can't accomplish what I set out to do. There's simply no room in my life for people who tell me to get real or that I'm dreaming.

Whenever I'm told that something is impossible or something simply can't be done, I just smile and say, "Watch me."

Their negativity then fuels my desire to prove them wrong. I guess my dad knew this and knew how to push the right buttons to get the best possible outcome.

> **"Being realistic is the most commonly traveled road to mediocrity."**
> **– Will Smith**

---

6   "Ericsson Mobility Report: 90 percent will have a mobile phone by 2020," Ericsson, 2014, http://www.ericsson.com/news/1872291.

My Takeaway for this chapter:

When people tell you that you cant do something or to be realistic, understand that it is more about them than you. Their issues, their failures, and their lack of will to achieve their goals in life.

The moment you realize their negativity is because they're unhappy with their own lives, you will no longer feel bad about yourself!

Chapter 12: 100% and No Less

"I've got a theory that if you give 100% all
of the time, somehow things will work out
in the end."
– Larry Bird

Are You a Winner?

Professional athletes are exceptionally gifted people. Not only do they have to be nearly perfect at their chosen sports, but they also have to deal with the world's media constantly hounding them. If you make a mistake at work, it often gets overlooked. However, if a professional athlete makes a mistake, it is broadcast across the Internet within moments. The reason professional athletes earn the big bucks is that they rise above these setbacks and manage to come back and perform at the highest level. Individuals don't rise above the crowd by accident, no matter what their endeavor – when they rise, it's because they possess qualities that other people don't. Here is some food for thought on becoming a top achiever.

Heart

Every human being has a physical heart, but rare are those who possess a heart for success. This heart is a combination of two very powerful inclinations: **internal motivation** and **work ethic**.

Many people believe that they are internally motivated, but lack the work ethic to give it all they have. Others work extremely hard, but are motivated for the wrong reasons. Natural athletes may possess more skill than a person who is internally motivated; however, natural athletes who lack sufficient internal motivation and/or work ethic will never be a match for the person who has passion for what they want to do.

> **"You know, the Greeks didn't write obituaries;**
> **they only asked one question after a man died.**
> **'Did he live with passion?'"**
> **– *Serendipity***

Work Ethic

Top achievers have an unbelievable work ethic. They are willing to sacrifice other pleasures in order to achieve their desired goals. As a soldier, the work you perform – a combination of physical and mental effort – is focused and intense. Achievers must focus on their goals and develop a strategy to obtain those goals, very rarely deviating from their planned path.

Absorbed

Being absorbed doesn't mean concentrating on an individual object, but rather becoming totally focused on what you are doing. Every now and again, the average person attending the gym will finish a workout, look at the clock, and wonder where the time went. Being totally into what you are doing is quality time, and top achievers are in this state more than others.

Fun

Having fun might not seem to fit into the rest of the plan, but enjoyment is essential to accomplishing what you aim to achieve. It is human nature to repeat those things that make us feel good, whether they are in or out of our comfort zones.

Add these ingredients together, and you have produced a person who is conscious of where he or she is at and where he or she wants to go.

"A winner is someone who recognizes his God-given talents, works his tail off to develop them into skills, and uses these skills to accomplish his goals."
– Larry Bird

The Two-Week Challenge That Will Change Your Life.

I was 24 years of age. I had just finished a five-kilometer run and was standing outside of the gym in the army barracks having a stretch.

A sergeant whom I respected came up to me and said, "Hey, Ritch, what did you just do?"

I said, "I've just finished a five-kilometer run."

"What time did you do?" he asked me, and then crossed his arms, like he was waiting to be impressed.

I told him that I finished in 22 minutes. He asked me if I could've done it faster.

I said, "Yeah, sure. I guess I could've done it in 18 minutes."

His arms still crossed, he asked, "Then why didn't you?"

I struggled to find a reply, and he continued,

"I've been watching you for the last three weeks, and one thing I have noticed is you do just enough. You do just enough to get by. Just enough to tick the boxes."

After this backhanded scolding and being put in my place, I realized I was lost for words and that he was right.

"Will you do me a favor over the next two weeks?" he asked.

Having a great amount of respect for this man, I agreed and started to listen to his request.

"Every single thing you do, everything – I want you to put your heart, mind, and soul even into the smallest acts and give 100% effort in everything."

I told him I could do that, no problem.

That night, I was lying in bed and I thought about the conversation we'd had. I thought, *As of tomorrow, I'll give this 100% and I'll see how it goes.*

Every single thing I did – whether it was buttering a piece of toast, making my bed, even the smallest acts – I gave 100% and nothing less, and that was when my life changed. That was when, all of a sudden, I started to become a better soldier. I started to become better in every single thing I did, and I started to stand out from my peers. I started to win awards because in every single thing that I did, I gave 100% and started to stand out from everyone else. Soon enough, that became a habit, and it was a very good habit I got into.

That one conversation both changed and revolutionized my life.

> **"Success is not in our nature; it's in our habits."**
> **– George Marcus**

The Habit of Success

Why did my life change after I gave 100% in everything I did? Because I took action. In my motivational presentations, I hold up a $50 note and ask, "Who wants this $50 note?" The audience laughs and takes it as a joke.

I ask them who wants it again and again, and they laugh and then begin to look at one another until the penny drops and at least one of them stands up and runs to the front of the room to grab it from my hand.

At this point, I tell them that it's not a trick and the $50 is theirs to keep.

Then I ask the rest of the participants, "What did that one person do that no one else did?"

The answer is simple. They got off of their ass (GOYA) and took action. They did what was necessary to get the job done, and that is exactly what you must do if you want to succeed in life. It's no good having goals if you're all talk and no action. Taking action is the key.

I then ask the group, "How many of you thought about getting up and grabbing the money, but something stopped you? The only reason we don't take action is because of fear. Now try to remember what was going through your head that stopped you from standing up."

The usual answers are, "I didn't want to look like I needed it" or "I didn't need it that badly," "I wasn't sure if you were really going to give it to me," "I was too far back in the room," "Other people need it more than I do," "I didn't want to look greedy," "I was afraid I might be doing something wrong and people might judge me."

Whatever the excuses were that stopped them from getting out of their seats are probably the same things they say to themselves in everyday life as excuses to stop them from achieving their goals.

> **"Don't give me the labor pains . . .
> just give me the baby."**
> **– Unknown**

Don't be one of those left wondering why you didn't jump up and claim that $50 note. Make sure you rise to the level of your abilities instead of falling to the level of your excuses.

I want to issue you a challenge over the next 14 days. Analyze your actions and what you say to yourself. You should notice that on a regular basis, you come up with excuses and reasons why you can't do something. As soon as you stop making excuses and talking yourself out of things, your life will change for the better.

> **"The only thing standing between you and your goal is the bullshit story you keep telling yourself as to why you can't achieve it."**
> **– Jordon Belfort**

My Takeaway for this chapter:

GOYA!! I dare you to take the two-week challenge! Put 100% effort into everything you do for the next two weeks and then watch how your life changes for the better.

Chapter 13: What Advice Would You Give Your Younger Self?

"Don't regret growing older.
It's a privilege denied to many."
– Unknown

Today is your 90th birthday. Your family and close friends have decided to throw you a milestone party to celebrate. As the party starts to taper off, you spot a person you don't recognize and walk over and introduce yourself. The man appears to be around 70 years of age, has a receding hairline and grey hair that resembles Albert Einstein's, and keys to a DeLorean.[7]

The man tells you he has invented a time machine that can transport you back in time to when you were 15 years old. He says that you will have 30 minutes to spend with your adolescent self. What advice would you give your younger self?

Thinking about the advice we would give our younger selves can influence us in our present lives and enable us to live more happily today.

This is something I think you will benefit from. After you read this chapter, I would like you to sit down and invest 10 minutes in writing down what lessons you would impart. Then spend another 5-10 minutes reflecting on whether you are able to incorporate those lessons into your current life. Listen carefully to the advice you would give your younger self, as there is a message in there trying to get out. I have completed the same exercise, and this is what guidance I would offer:

- You were born with a gift. Once you find that gift – and listen very carefully to your intuition and gut instinct, as it will guide you – it is important to give that gift away. At times, your head will lead you one way and your heart another. Don't suppress your instincts; your gut is right more times than not.

---

7   i.e. the car used as a time machine in *Back to the Future*.

- Those sleepless nights worrying about how it will all work out are a waste, especially with the things that are out of your control. Focus on the things you can control and not on the ones you can't. Pay attention to the things that impact you directly and not to those that don't. Preparation in everything you do is the cornerstone of confidence, which in turn is your foundation for success.

- Believe in yourself, in your worth. Chase your dreams; they can be reality. If your passion and desire are strong enough, you can achieve anything.

- Countless people don't live; they simply exist. They are happy to act like sheep, follow the crowd, and react to their surroundings rather than look for what they want in life. They invest so much time trying to fit in and be accepted, they never listen to their gut instincts and intuition and find who they are inside.

> **"Always trust your first gut instinct.**
> **If you feel that something is wrong, it usually**
> **is."**
> **– Unknown**

- The majority of people keep their passions constrained (normally behind closed doors where nobody can see or judge them), only allowing others slight glimpses when their surroundings appear safe to do so.

- Many people spend 8-10 hours a day in jobs they detest, primarily motivated by money that will allow them to buy things they don't really need. They go to places they don't really like, to impress people they don't enjoy being around. They constantly compare themselves to other people. Their life revolves around what society dictates is best for them instead of following their passions.

- Passion is energy. Passion is the driving force for success. Optimism and positive energy are triggered by passion. You will only be happy when you do what you love. Passion is happiness!

- Passion is the true motivation, and it is passion that keeps you going in this hard, competitive world. You will succeed in life when what you do is in harmony with who you are. In turn, you'll be naturally energized by doing it.

- Doing what you love and finding your purpose will be the things that motivate you to get out of bed in the morning and to look forward to the day ahead. When your work or business complements your personality, you are always going to succeed.

"Your time is limited, so don't waste it living someone else's life. Don't be trapped by dogma – which is living with the results of other people's thinking. Don't let the noise of others' opinions drown out your own inner voice. And most importantly, have the courage to follow your heart and intuition. They somehow already know what you truly want to become. Everything else is secondary."

– Steve Jobs

- Don't get so busy making a living that you forget how to make a life. Take time to reflect, and connect with those who make you feel good and whom you enjoy being around. Maintaining a balance without being constantly fatigued from the treadmill of a work existence is the secret to happiness.

- Fulfill every dream, and travel while you are young. As you get older, your health and recovery time won't be what they used to be. Good health brings an independence very few recognize until they no longer have it.

- No one is coming to rescue you. It's up to you to create whatever life you want. Whatever has to be done, it is you, and only you, who can take responsibility and make it happen.

"The first eighteen years of your life are like a free trial, and after that it's pay to play."
- Unknown

- Persistence and tenacity are valued attributes, but sometimes it is more important to know when to give up. With our social and cultural influences and the way our brains work, we tend to be extremely persistent. The threat of failure often drives you to work towards unattainable and impossible goals. Being a quitter or giving up on something often may not be perceived as the best traits, but sidelining unachievable goals early can free you up to work on something better.

- The human brain is persistent and enduring. Even when the more lucrative alternative would be giving up, there is this social and cultural pressure to avoid being called a "quitter." The age-old proverb "Try and try till you succeed" does not fit into today's competitive world – in years past, maybe. Although we now know that persistence is the most valuable asset we can have, it is also important to know when to call it quits.

"Nothing in the world can take the place of persistence.

Talent will not; nothing is more common than unsuccessful men with talent.

Genius will not; unrewarded genius is almost a proverb.

Education will not; the world is full of educated derelicts.

Persistence and determination alone are omnipotent."

– Calvin Coolidge (US President, 1923-1929)

- In times of adversity, be resilient. Know that deep down you are strong and you will always come out on the other side. Your track record for getting through bad days is 100%, and that's pretty good.

"The world ain't all sunshine and rainbows. It's a very mean and nasty place . . . and it don't care how tough you are; it will beat you to your knees and keep you there permanently if you let it. You, me, or nobody is gonna hit as hard as life. But it ain't about how hard you're hit. . . . It's about how hard you can get hit, and keep moving forward . . . how much you can take, and keep moving forward. That's how winning is done. Now, if you know what you're worth, go out and get what you're worth. But you gotta be willing to take the hits. And not pointing fingers saying: You ain't what you wanna be because of him or her or anybody. Cowards do that, and that ain't you!"

– Sylvester Stallone, *Rocky 6*

- People are going to try very hard to change you, to break your spirit. Don't allow others to impose their fears and limitations on your dreams. You don't require other people's recognition, approval, or opinions to be successful. Use their pessimism as ammunition to achieve your ambition.

- Whatever you wish to achieve in life, chances are someone has already done it. All you have to do is take their formula, make it your own, and then look for your own unique point of difference. If you are frightened to be yourself, you will end up working for someone who isn't.

- Don't be afraid of failing. Society will dictate and reinforce failure as a negative; however, society is wrong. Fail often and learn from your mistakes. That's the way you grow and move forward.

- This life is a beautiful gift, so get out there and live it. Experience it. Make mistakes. Forgive yourself for your mistakes. Keep an open mind and learn to listen. Anyone can talk, but not many people can listen.

- Don't be afraid of change. Change is part of life. It triggers progress and is necessary in order for us to grow. Every change you experience is a turning page. Changes will bring new beginnings and excitement to your life.

"For the past 33 years, I have looked in the mirror every morning and asked myself: 'If today were the last day of my life, would I want to do what I am about to do today?' And whenever the answer has been 'No' for too many days in a row, I know I need to change something."
– Steve Jobs

- Tell the people close to you how you feel. Don't be afraid to express your feelings. Don't allow your friendships and close family ties to deteriorate. Anyone can go at any time, and you may not get that chance again.

- Don't settle for just anything in life. You deserved to have everything in life just the way you want it. From this point on, the attitude of just settling needs to stop. You must take control of even the smallest details in your life, and once you do that, you will see things change for the better. By speaking up and not settling for whatever you are given will ensure that you are in control.

- Life isn't always going to work out the way you have planned – but sometimes it works out better. Be kind and show empathy to people, and when something good happens in your life, it is your responsibility to send the elevator back down to someone who needs a lift up.

"Never forget that you are one of a kind. Never forget that if there weren't any need for you in all your uniqueness to be on this earth, you wouldn't be here in the first place. And never forget, no matter how overwhelming life's challenges and problems seem to be, that one person can make a difference in the world. In fact, it is always because of one person that all the changes that matter in the world come about. So be that one person. "
– Buckminster Fuller

My Takeaway for this chapter:

What do you spend hours reading about? When I get passionate about something, I'll read about it for hours on end. I'll buy books and magazines. I'll spend days on the Internet finding out more. There may be a few possibilities here for you . . . and all of them are possible career paths. Don't close your mind to these topics. Look into them.

Chapter 14: Life is a Gift. Never Take It for Granted.

"If you have food in your fridge, clothes on your back, a roof over your head, and a place to sleep, you are richer than 75% of the world.

If you have money in the bank, your wallet, and some spare change, you are among the top 8% of the world's wealthy.

If you woke up this morning with more health than illness, you are more blessed than the million people who will not survive this week.

If you have never experienced the danger of battle, the agony of imprisonment or torture, or the horrible pangs of starvation, you are luckier than 500 million people alive and suffering.

If you can read this message, you are more fortunate than 3 billion people in the world who cannot read it at all."

– Unknown

Autopilot

A recent research by a former professor of medicine at Stanford University suggests that 95% of our choices, actions, emotions, and behavior comes from the programming in our subconscious minds. The same research shows that the conscious mind provides 5% or less, depending on the individual, of our conscious awareness during the day.

Without realizing it, people live large chunks of their lives on autopilot and take most things for granted. Most of us wake up every morning without giving a second thought to the fact that we are alive – that our heart continues beating and our lungs keep filling with air without us having to do a thing.

We get out of bed, head to the shower, or get ready for work without considering how our subconscious mind is controlling our walking, coordination, and dexterity.

We prioritize our days, manage our appointments and tasks without recognizing the value of the good people around us, without knowing how fortunate we are to have food in the fridge, clothes on our back, a roof over our head, and a place to sleep.

We overlook and take so much for granted in our life, only missing things when they're gone. Sometimes we require a wake-up call – normally an illness or the death of someone close to us.

When that happens, all of a sudden you become a patient in a world of waiting rooms, sometimes waiting hours for a result; attending appointment after appointment and spending too much time in cold, clinical machines like MRIs & CTs; kneeling at the base of a hospital bed, praying for miracles; and dealing with the frustration of tests and examinations.

Then you look at the healthy people skipping down the street like you once did, you realize you took it all for granted, and you wish you could do it all again and have your time over.

> **"Most of the people who died yesterday had plans for today. Never take life for granted."**
> **– Unknown**

My Wake-Up Calls

In 1996, I was on a promotional course serving in the Australian Army when I was told of what was and what still is Australia's largest ever peacetime disaster: 18 soldiers were killed when two Black Hawk helicopters collided during a live-fire training exercise. Many of the soldiers were guys I'd not only worked with but shared social time with as well. They were my friends.

This accident caused a great deal of sorrow and anguish for the majority of the Australian Defence Force. It made everyone realize their time could be up in the blink of an eye. I remember dealing with the issue and thinking that I must no longer take anything or anyone for granted. I remember thinking, *What if on the morning of the accident, one of the boys had an argument or refused to kiss his wife or partner goodbye? He didn't realize that this was going to be the last time they saw each other.*

We take it for granted that our loved ones are coming home to us, that we'll get a chance to say goodbye, to tell them how much they mean to us.

The trouble is, you think you have time.
– Buddha

Another wake-up call for me was a close friend of mine, Sam, who had the world at his feet. He was 23 years old and was to marry the love of his life in three months' time. He had just finished his degree in accountancy and secured a job at a well-known and reputable firm. He was a good-looking young guy and had the type of personality that drew people in; everyone wanted to be around him. He was an amazingly talented athlete in numerous sports and played golf off a 3 handicap after only playing the sport for 18 months, all without a golfing lesson.

Sam, two other close friends, and I played golf religiously every Sunday. On Sunday 14th February 2010, we decided to cancel golf due to a few of us having family commitments.

Sam set off and played in a charity soccer day for his new employers. Not surprisingly, he starred during the game, scoring numerous goals and saving a few as well.

Then, after what seemed to be a routine header, he felt nauseated and started to experience a headache. He went to the sidelines and approached the medical staff, who advised him to sip on water, saying he was probably suffering from dehydration. Sam knew that it wasn't dehydration; it just didn't feel right.

Sam's headache continued to worsen to the point where an ambulance was called and Sam was taken to the hospital. As the ambulance pulled up to the accident and emergency room, Sam's eyes rolled to the back of his head, and right there and then, he suffered eight strokes.

Sam's life has never been the same, and there is a high probability that he will never recover completely. This was yet another wake-up call for me: it again made me realize that we will not be here for a long time and that life is too short for regrets. We have to be conscious of being grateful for things that we have; if we concentrate on what we don't have, we will never have enough.

"Understand your worth. Value your life.
Appreciate your blessings."
– Unknown

Not taking anything for granted also helps you to put things in their proper perspective. When an obstacle or adversity creeps into your day, keep in mind that every difficulty happens for a reason.

By this alignment, we become happier and more engaged in the process of the law of attraction.

I have learned that gratitude is one of the most important virtues. Each night, just before going to sleep, I think of three things that I am grateful for. This has profoundly altered my perspective and the quality of my life.

"The happiest people don't necessarily have
the best of everything, but they make the most
out of everything."
– Sam Cawthorn

My Takeaway for this chapter:

When you next pay a bill, be sure to write down something positive that the product or service has helped you accomplish by using it. It will teach you to shift your focus from money going out and being taken away, to seeing the value of the product or service you are receiving.

Chapter 15: Be the Hero of Your Own Story

"Courage is contagious. When a brave
man takes a stand, the spines of others are
often stiffened."
– Billy Graham

The Design of a Hero

Having spent a quarter of my life in the army and having witnessed firsthand some of the most heroic men and women serving their country, I have always asked myself, "What does a hero look like?"

A great many of the people whom I served with and respect the opinion of would collectively reserve the term "hero" for select individuals. The term "hero" is defended for those who act in the face of danger or adversary while showing courage; they do what is morally right in spite of peer pressure. A hero is defined by his or her choices and actions, not by chance or circumstances that arise.

A hero can be brave and willing to sacrifice his life, but I think we all have a hero in us – someone who is unselfish and without want of reward, who is determined to help others. My heroes are people like my family members, who have stood by me and supported me through thick and thin; my school teachers, who didn't give up on and believed in me although the time they invested didn't guarantee results; and a mentor, who led the way and took the time to steer me in the right direction when I was lost.

I've learned most heroes are ordinary people – it is their act that is extraordinary.

We all have a unique talent and skill set. What the world needs is heroes who have the ability to make extraordinary things happen in the environment we live in.

Performing an act of kindness or good deed, no matter how small, starts a shift of positive energy that can profoundly change lives. Doing something nice for someone with no ulterior motive can impact someone's life and give them hope for the future.

A good deed you did for someone today can have a far-reaching, powerful, and lasting effect on more than just you and that person.

How you affect others allows you to be the hero of your own story and sets an example of what is possible. You become an inspiration, opening the awareness of others to their own potential.

> **"Be kind, for everyone you meet is fighting a hard battle."**
> **– Plato**

One Good Deed Deserves Another

I remember travelling from Heathrow airport back to Australia. I was waiting in a lengthy line to check in. I had arrived several hours beforehand and decided to check in early, go through airport security checks, and wait there until we boarded.

One thing I like to do in my spare time is people watch. While I was in this line for a good 45 minutes, I noticed numerous people in front of me checking in and the charades that went on between each staff member and the passengers ready to depart.

What caught my eye was how most people were just going through the motions and were generally unappreciative of the job the ground staff was doing to get them home. Yes, the staff members were getting paid to do their job, but a bit of courtesy doesn't cost you anything – and, as we all know, you can catch more flies with honey than with vinegar.

While scanning the counters that were administrating and checking people in, through the organized chaos, I heard a faint English accent say, "Next." As I looked up, I noticed someone ushering me down; I was next in line.

I got to the counter, and the lady serving me asked, as she had a hundred times before, "Hi, how are you?"

I said, "I'm good, thanks, but more importantly, how are you?"

Her eyes shifted from checking and scanning my passport, which she had taken from the counter, to looking up at me with surprise and amazement. She said,

"I'm good, thanks. And thanks for asking."

Although she was extremely busy, I wanted to take her mind off the job just for a minute and make her feel like she was human again – and not just some machine like person that herded cattle to a destination.

"Been a long day?" I asked.

"Almost eight hours," she replied. "All without a break yet."

She looked tired and on the verge of losing her will to live after eight hours of dealing with complaints from passengers trying to talk their way out of excess baggage charges and into seating upgrades.

"Once we are done here and before I go through the departure gate, can I offer to buy you a coffee – seeing as though you haven't had a break all day?" I asked.

The lady looked up once again, squinting. That same look of amazement came over her face, and she said, "That would be lovely; thank you very much. I could use a coffee right about now."

"How do you have it?" I asked.

"A latte would be fantastic."

So after we finalized the check-in details, I went over and bought her a café latte for £2.50. I gave her a *Be You. Be Great.* Act of Kindness card as well.

It was the least I could do to show my appreciation for her getting me home safe and sound. You could tell by the expression on her face that she was sincerely grateful and surprised that a stranger would do such a thing.

"Use that card and do something nice for someone else," I commented.

She smiled, thanked me, and wished me a great flight.

Then as I was walking away, I heard, "Next," this time with an enthusiasm that was contagious. I looked back and noticed a smile that surely would make the next passenger feel like he or she was dealing with someone in high spirits and with a newfound faith in humanity.

> **"You never know when a moment and a few sincere words can have an impact on a life forever."**
> **– Zig Ziglar**

Free Parking

I was in an annual general meeting in the city. It was running overtime, and the deadline for my on-street parking was approaching. I needed to excuse myself so I could feed the meter to avoid a parking fine.

I ran up the street with only minutes remaining until the meter expired. As I was approaching my car, I noticed a parking officer looking at the license plate and registration details of the car directly behind mine. I approached him and explained my situation.

"Excuse me. A close friend and I are currently in a meeting, and the meeting has run over. This is his car, and the one in front is mine. I am just wondering if I could possibly pay and extend both his and my parking?"

The officer looked at his watch, looked at the car, thought about it for a second, and agreed and walked off toward an adjoining street as the remainder of the car spaces were vacant. I put an additional few dollars in the meter for both cars, then placed the ticket in my car and under the windshield wiper of the car behind me.

This wasn't a friend's car. This car belonged to a complete stranger, a person I had never met, but I didn't want him or her to receive a fine. So I put the ticket under the wiper as well as a *Be You. Be Great.* Acts of Kindness card and left the rest to fate.

When the person arrived back at his car, he would have noticed a ticket with additional time added to it as well as the Acts of Kindness card and hopefully, being grateful and appreciative, paid it forward, perpetuating the cycle and helping numerous people.

> **"I shall pass through this world but once. Any good therefore that I can do or any kindness that I can show to any human being, let me do it now. Let me not defer or neglect it, for I shall not pass this way again."**
> **– Mahatma Gandhi**

Saving the World

Think back to a time in your life when someone was a hero for you. I bet you have never forgotten what they did for you, their courage, and their actions.

A hero is not necessarily someone who wears a cape, has superpowers, and saves the world.

Being a hero is about helping others and endeavoring to make a difference in other people's lives, creating a ripple effect that all started with you.

Believe it or not, helping others is more about helping ourselves than about the people we are helping. We gain increased self-esteem, self-confidence, and pride from knowing we are doing the right thing and making a difference.

> **"Too often we underestimate the power of a touch, a smile, a kind word, a listening ear, an honest compliment, or the smallest act of caring, all of which have the potential to turn a life around."**
> **– Leo Buscaglia**

My Takeaway for this chapter:

Endeavour to be a good person and practice doing good Deeds for other people for no reason. It is a natural high that you will enjoy and no doubt want to repeat.

Chapter 16: Trade Your Expectations for Appreciation and Your Whole World Changes

"Be happy with what you have while
working for what you want."
– Helen Keller

An Attitude of Gratitude

On beyoubegreat.net, I have started an initiative entitled **No Negatives**. The objective is to not complain, criticize, or gossip for seven days in a row. I believe that if you can improve your choice of words and how you communicate with yourself, your thoughts and actions will follow. How you interact with yourself influences the choices you make, which in turn inspires action.

Being grateful and appreciative of what you have in life changes your focus from what you want to what you already have. Recent research suggests that growth in many areas of your life can result from the practice of gratitude. Being thankful can not only increase happiness, but it can also improve your immune system and health through reducing stress. It enriches both personal and social relationships, and allows us to perceive and deal with adversities and setbacks with greater ease.

> **"Gratitude turns what we have into enough."**
> **– Melody Beattie**

No Negatives also calls for your complete attention and asks you to imagine losing a variety of things that you take for granted each day, such as the roof over your head, your ability to see or smell, your ability to breathe, and anything else that provides comfort. Then, every day, envision getting each of these things back and try to appreciate how lucky you are to have them. By doing an exercise like this, you begin discovering contentment in little things rather than searching for bigger milestones. This ensures you appreciate the good that is already present in your life.

> **"Happiness is an inside job."**
> **– William Arthur Ward**

Adjusting your mindset and how you perceive things enables you to put matters in the proper perspective. No one is immune from obstacles or adversity, but by living with gratitude and looking inwardly at everything you have, you start to realize that the forefather of self-help, Napoleon Hill, had it right when he said, "Every adversity, every failure, every heartache carries with it the seed of an equal or greater benefit."

So, when you're next faced with a disappointment or a setback, or things are not going according to plan, ask yourself, **"What else could this mean?"** and **"How can I grow or learn from this?"**

A good example is how my wife and I dealt with the disappointment of not being able to conceive a child. Within a four-year window, we had five unsuccessful attempts at in vitro fertilization and had front-row seats on the emotional, physical, and financial rollercoaster. It took its toll on our lives, but through this adversity, we realized that nothing could take away what we already had, and that was each other.

When our fifth and final attempt was unsuccessful, and after what felt like an eternity experiencing a variety of complicated emotions and crushing disappointments, including a miscarriage, we drew a line in the sand and agreed that we could not stay or live in this negative mindset. We realized we have a great deal to be thankful for and that we shouldn't be concentrating on what we don't have but rather on what we do have in our lives: we are blessed with a loving family and great friends.

> **"If you concentrate on what you don't have, you will never, ever have enough."**
> **– Oprah Winfrey**

Don't Waste Your Time with Anxiety: Tips from a Sufferer

Rather than wasting your most valuable asset waiting for a positive experience in order to feel thankful, try noticing the smaller things as well as the good in bad situations. Once you can master this, you will be able to appreciate the things you previously took for granted.

The person who decides to be grateful is less likely to be depressed, jealous, lonely, or anxious. Recent research on depression and anxiety suggests that anxiety is the most common of all mental disorders and currently affects about one in 13 people globally, which is 7.3%.[8] If you spend a fair amount of time worrying about the future, regretting the past, or reliving an argument that ended long ago, you may fit into this category. You need to understand that you are not on your own and that millions of other people are going through and worrying about similar things. As I have previously suffered from high levels of anxiety, the advice I wish to offer is first hand and something that has worked for me.

I found that I was dwelling on the past and allowing my mind to wander, which is a prescription for feeling anxious. Thanks to a friend's advice, I realized the things I was anxious about were not in front of me or real right now. I needed to start focusing on the here and now. As soon as I started to practice that and it became a habit, I became happier.

When something good occurred, I attempted to capture my mindset and what I was thinking. It was only then that I began to realize that I was not actually enjoying or

8   A. J. Baxter, K. M. Scott, T. Vos and H. A. Whiteford (2013). "Global prevalence of anxiety disorders: a systematic review and meta-regression," *Psychological Medicine*, 43, pp 897-910.

paying attention to the moment and the good, but more so focusing on where it could lead and what was going to happen next. By creating this awareness and slowing down to appreciate the moment, you will notice a decrease in depression and an increase in happiness.

> **"Plenty of people miss their share of happiness,**
> **not because they never found it,**
> **but because they didn't stop to enjoy it."**
> **– William Feather**

Every day, I wake up and am given a choice: I can be grateful for what I have and make the most of it, or I can complain and focus on the things I don't have, which leads to feeling depressed. An attitude of gratitude is not concluding that everything in our lives is perfect – it just means we are aware of the good things and the blessings we have.

> **"Man surprised me most about humanity**
> **because he sacrifices his health in order to**
> **make money.**
>
> **Then he sacrifices money to recuperate his**
> **health. And then he is so anxious about the**
> **future that he does not enjoy the present; the**
> **result being that he does not live in the present**
> **or the future; he lives as if he is never going to**
> **die, and then dies having never really lived."**
> **– His Holiness the 14th Dalai Lama**

My Takeaway for this chapter:

Carry a gratitude rock in your pocket or purse. I carry one in my wallet. This rock is a reminder for me to catch my mindset and be thankful for something right at that moment. I carry it with me wherever I

go. The idea is simple and serves as a reminder to not focus on what you don't have but rather on what you do have.

Go to www.beyoubegreat.net and download the complimentary infographic on my 12 steps to happiness and place it on your fridge or office notice board.

An easy-to-remember acronym is ACT. Apply ACT to each and every aspect of your life.

A = Appreciation. Think of showing appreciation and gratitude like a bank account. The more gratitude you show and the more appreciation you build up, the greater your wealth of happiness, health, and successful relationships.

C = Compliment. My brother used to tell me that an honest compliment doesn't hurt or cost you anything. Giving a compliment is a sign of respect and increases our own capacity for gratitude.

T = That's Why I Love You (TWILY). Start a TWILY journal and write daily, weekly, or even monthly. You can invest fewer than five minutes of your time and still encourage a mindset shift and create a habit of looking for the good in others rather than the negatives. Writing a TWILY journal will assist you to create and share positive, loving, and reaffirming thoughts for those who are most important in your life.

Chapter 17: The Present Moment Is All You Will Ever Have

"If you are depressed, you are living in the past.
If you are anxious, you are living in the future.
If you are at peace, you are living in the
present."
– Lao Tzu

We Live in the Information Age

The age of distraction and interruption.

I have noticed that my life has become a continuous supply of information, advice, noise, emails, texts, social media, and more TV channels than I know what to do with. Two separate studies in 2012 suggest that over 90% of smart phone users in the United States admit to their device being within arm's length at all times.[9] The power of the Internet is available in almost every country in the world, with the last five years amassing more scientific data than we have from the entire history of mankind before that.

Research suggests that the average person has gone from being exposed to about 500 signs and advertisements a day in the 1970s to as many as 5,000 a day today. Every diversion and distraction has the same goal: get our attention and engage us. Because of this, our ability to concentrate and focus on a singular thing becomes increasingly difficult.

Our minds never stop. We daydream and conjure up visions of exotic locations to visit and dream homes to own. We look at our watches and two seconds later forget the time. We walk into a room and forget why we are there. We recall and reflect on past memories, all without appreciating and spending time in the present. It's as if our minds are in one time zone and our bodies in another. Buddhism refers to this as having a "monkey mind" – a mind in which your thoughts leap and jump around in your head, like monkeys swinging from tree to tree.

---

9   According to Arbitron and Edison Research survey results in April 2012.

Meditation or mindfulness is a great way of switching off that flow of thoughts, changing the conversations in your head, and silencing those monkeys.

> **"Meditation is not a way of making your mind quiet. It's a way of entering into the quiet that's already there – buried under the 50,000 thoughts the average person thinks every day."**
> **– Deepak Chopra**

Mindfulness is basically being conscious of and paying attention to the here and now. It is all about slowing down and giving no energy to the thoughts and chitchat going on in your head. It is acknowledgement and appreciation of the moment you are in. If you take the time to appreciate what you are doing in the present, regardless of how small the act may be, you start to feel contentment, and the world does not seem so frantic.

Striving for mindfulness is not about competing with anyone else or even about trying to improve yourself – it is purely a matter of paying attention to your immediate experience. This is living in the moment. This is my reset button, a place where nothing else matters and nothing happens next. When you practice mindfulness, it is as if the world has stopped while you recharge your batteries.

Right now. This very second. This instant. What are you observing?

Start by sitting and concentrating on your breath. As you are reading this book and your concentration is on every word that is written, stop for a second and focus your attention on drawing your next breath, its length, and the way it flows in and out of your nostrils. Sounds boring, right? But stick with it, and with persistence, you will find your attention and awareness improve. This will greatly assist your concentration, which can go astray in the fast-paced and distraction-filled lives we lead.

> **"I have known a great many troubles,**
> **but most of them never happened."**
> **– Mark Twain**

We have all heard the saying "Stop and smell the roses." What does this saying mean?

It means that we should take time to appreciate what is going on around us. As we get older and are able to look back on our lives in hindsight, we sometimes regret not appreciating "something" or "someone." Most of us think we are not good enough, compare ourselves to everyone around us, and, worst of all, worry that things won't go according to plan and that we'll mess them up.

Too often in life, we concentrate on what we need to do and where we are headed rather than appreciate where we are and whom we are with. If we can remember that we are human beings and not human doings and allocate a small percentage of our day to appreciating silence and calm, we will be happier and more relaxed.

> **"You should sit in meditation for 20 minutes**
> **a day, unless you're too busy; then you should**
> **sit for an hour."**
> **– old Zen adage**

Don't get me wrong here: this is not an easy feat. Regardless of how much you practice, you will still have thoughts popping into your head uninvited. The objective of mindfulness is not to eliminate all thoughts (since thinking is what our brains do best) but to teach you how to respond to and what energy to give those thoughts.

My visualization and approach is to think of thoughts as clouds passing by from one side of my mind to the other, giving them no energy and, consequently, no impact.

Mindfulness is not just about calming the mind and reducing stress; it also offers a host of other benefits that amateur and professional athletes, soldiers returning from active duty, and physically and mentally fatigued toilers in the corporate world are finding beneficial. These benefits include reduced anxiety levels, lower blood pressure, minimal sleeping problems, and decreased symptoms of anger, hostility, and depression.

One of the trademarks of depression is the fear of what will happen next. This fear is not living in the present moment; it is worrying about the future. Such fear can become a habit and a fixed mental state and is associated with numerous stress-related health problems. Concentrating on the present moment helps to alleviate this fear and worry as we invariably feel safe and composed in the now.

With their origins emerging from Asia and filtering through to Western culture, and with their increase in popularity and mainstream status over the past decade, mindfulness and meditation seem to be here to stay.

By meditating and practicing mindfulness, you not only give yourself the permission to slow down and recharge, but you also give yourself permission to be more receptive than reactive. Your technique is secondary to your intention.

My Takeaway for this chapter:

Imagine working throughout the day without a chance to eat and refuel your body. We eat to replenish and maintain energy. Time to refuel and replenish the mind.

I suggest fitting these two practices into your day:

Quick snack: take 30-60 seconds twice a day subject to opportunity.

Main meal: take 5 minutes once a day after having completed one activity and before beginning another.

Sit in a chair so that your spine is upright and balanced but relaxed. Allow your eyes to gently close. Now, move your attention gently through each step. Be conscious of your body and its connection with the chair.

Sit comfortably and focus your energy on your body. Start with your head and work your way down to your toes, concentrating on each individual body part separately and clearing thoughts that pop into your head. Remember, mindfulness isn't about getting somewhere. It is simply about knowing where you already are.

After a time, let your attention move to your listening. Hear whatever sounds there are to hear without analyzing them. Once again, if thoughts come, let them pass.

Chapter 18: STRESSED Spelled Backwards is DESSERTS

"Worrying does not take away tomorrow's troubles. It takes away today's peace."
– Randy Armstrong

Fight or Flight

When we are faced with a threat or a stressful situation, the response in our brains triggers us to either stand our ground (fight) or run (flight). "Fight or flight" is a phrase coined by Harvard University physiologist Walter Cannon back in the 1920s.

In any stressful or dangerous situation, a number of nerve cell responses ensure we are ready for the imminent scenario. To safeguard ourselves, the digestive system shuts down; alertness increases due to a rush of adrenaline and cortisol into the bloodstream; the heart rate increases and blood pressure rises; and breathing increases and becomes more rapid, providing more oxygen to larger muscles, preparing them to work harder.

All this happens in seconds. This hardwired response dates back to our primitive ancestors and is something we all use as a survival technique. Our early ancestors faced danger on a daily basis, and so, after millions of years of evolution, the fight or flight response is still alive and well in modern society.

I witnessed this firsthand during my time in the army, watching young soldiers constantly on edge with a fight or flight attitude. This happens in military operations from Vietnam to modern-day warzones such as Afghanistan and Iraq, where it is difficult to make a distinction between those who are fighting against you and those who are civilians. In many cases, civilians and enemy are deliberately amalgamated to cause confusion and uncertainty.

The fight or flight reaction to threats can be either perceived or real and sends our bodies into self-preservation mode.

Countless people live their life in a state of stress and, as a result, rarely experience relaxation. It is as if we are always preparing to stand and fight or run like hell even when there is no imminent threat. We worry that something bad may happen, and this keeps us in a state of unease.

> "Life is 10% what happens to you
> and 90% how you react to it."
> – Charles R. Swindoll

The human body is remarkable when its systems are in harmony and working together. If one system of the body does not perform or do its job, it can affect the rest of the body. Each night, when you go to sleep, your body repairs itself and endeavors to bring its systems back into harmony.

If your sleep is affected due to stress, worry, or a continued fight-or-flight state of hyperarousal, you are placing more stress and pressure on a body that's already battling with daytime tension. Your body's innate self-repair routine won't work efficiently if you remain stressed. Therefore, instead of waking fresh and renewed, stressed people become rundown and sick with the cycle perpetuating. This is fine and dandy when you are young and resilient; however, as we grow older, the requirement for a more undisturbed, settled sleep is essential.

Research suggests that stress is recognized as the primary cause for more than 60% of all illnesses and diseases.

Regardless of age or gender, the thing that triggers stress is feeling like you have minimal control but high levels of responsibility. This creates the perception of being trapped, of feeling like there is no way out of a particular situation. Link this with a constant feeling of things getting worse rather than better and a perceived diminishing social support network, and things quickly compound.

> **"Stress is not what happens to us.**
> **It's our response to what happens,**
> **and response is something we can choose."**
> **– Maureen Killoran**

The real problem lies in the fact that as human beings, we have fundamentally become addicted to stress. Most people have no idea and are oblivious to the fact that there are two primary kinds of stress: positive and negative.

Where these two differentiate is in duration and how you perceive them.

Negative stress is persistent and enduring, and therefore weakens your immune system and, more importantly, your resolve. Negative stress turns your thoughts and feelings inward so that you care more about yourself and getting relief from your stress than about others and helping to relieve their stress.

Examples of things that cause negative stress are unhappiness in your occupation, financial difficulties when there seems to be no way out and everything keeps piling up, navigating rush hour traffic, trying to make everyone else happy and having no time in your schedule to recharge, moving residences, the death or illness of someone you care about – basically, anything you would seek to avoid because it makes you unhappy and stressed.

The other side of the spectrum is positive stress. Positive stress is short and sharp and like a hit in the arm. It elicits an adrenaline response and stretches us to new limits. It helps us understand our talents and our limits so we can enjoy a better life.

Positive stress is a chemical cocktail that gives you a high. Adrenaline, serotonin, and endorphins are produced by our bodies and act like antidotes to the bad stress chemicals. I remember back in 1994, spending several weeks at the Army Parachute Training School, completing my basic parachute course. One particular day, we conducted six jumps back to back from 1,000 feet. I remember being in a heightened state of arousal. Like a kid in a theme park, I just wanted to go on the next ride. At the end of the day, we ate dinner together in the dining hall. A large majority of us were falling asleep due to the positive stress parachuting placed on our bodies and the high levels of adrenaline constantly released throughout the day. If you have not experienced parachuting or skydiving, think of a similar experience, such as activities like snowboarding, white water rafting, rock climbing, abseiling, bungee jumping, hang gliding, or even a scary ride at a theme park. All these adrenaline highs are addictive. They add stress to your body, but in a mostly positive way.

My Takeaway for this chapter:

Stress is physical, mental, and emotional.

Pushing yourself through regular exercise on a daily basis creates increased blood flow, which in turn allows your mind and body to work together.

Another great way to lower stress levels is to find something bigger than yourself. Look at any role model or pillar of the community, and you will notice that most of them spend time focused on activities

that are bigger than themselves. Find something you can aspire to that is worth more than the pain and suffering it causes. As Norman Vincent Peale once said, "The more you lose yourself in something bigger than yourself, the more energy you will have."

Next time you feel stressed, anxious, or overwhelmed, remember that there is always someone worse off than you. This mindset shift can certainly put whatever it is you're stressing over into perspective.

As a human being, you have a 100% chance of dying. You can't get better odds than that!

Remember when you were in high school and really nervous and stressed prior to a massive exam? What marks or results did you get? You probably can't remember. The message here is, don't allow yourself to get worked up over something that you probably won't remember in years to come.

Forget the "what ifs." Most of them never happen. What ifs consume you and take up vital mental energy. They will end up swallowing you like quick sand. The more you let your imagination run wild and think about the stress, the worse the scenarios play out in your head.

Chapter 19: 7-Day No Negatives Challenge

"Great minds discuss ideas;
average minds discuss events;
small minds discuss people."
– Eleanor Roosevelt

Be You. Be Great. 7-Day No Negatives Challenge

The *Be You. Be Great.* 7-Day No Negatives Challenge is designed to help train you to avoid complaining, criticizing, or gossiping for an entire week. It will be tough, but it will be rewarding as well.

I myself have completed the challenge on more than one occasion, and I found that by modifying my words, I am able to change my attitude and way of thinking. Your thoughts and words determine your emotions and how you react to certain situations. Unfortunately, complaining, criticizing, and gossiping are part of most people's lives – and most of the time, we are unconscious of it.

> **"Any fool can criticize, condemn, and complain – and most fools do."**
> **– Benjamin Franklin**

Our Default

The tendency to complain is a default habit and settles into our routines easily. It takes a real moment of honesty and clarity to even acknowledge we are doing it.

I would like to make a bold prediction before we start: participating and taking part in this challenge will cost you money. Having a minor monetary risk and being invested in achieving this goal will increase your motivation; otherwise, the challenge will fall by the wayside and won't have an impact.

You will need a No Negatives Jar and, from my experience, between $20-$50 in small denominations – a gold coin or a one dollar bill will suffice.

Now that you are cashed up, a conscious and more importantly an **HONEST** assessment must be made each time you complain, criticize, or gossip. Every time you catch yourself bitching or whining, put a dollar or two in the jar.

Your get-out-of-jail-free card is using the word "unless." You are allowed to use "unless" once a day.

This forces you to think of solutions when complaining. By using the word "unless," you are ultimately turning a negative complaint into a positive solution.

By completing the No Negatives 7-Day Challenge, you are on your way to forming a new and positive habit. Research suggests that it takes 21 days to form a habit, so if you feel yourself being negative about anything, feel free to start another 7-day challenge or even do the challenges consecutively.

After you have completed 7 days in a row of no complaining, criticizing, or gossiping, see how much money you have accumulated in your No Negatives Jar and offer that money, as well as the *Be You. Be Great.* Acts of Kindness card (found on the inside back cover of the book) to someone you think may appreciate it and pay it forward. The money used for the Act of Kindness can be diverse and ambiguous; it's completely up to you.

By involving yourself in *Be You. Be Great*'s Acts of Kindness, you are contributing to a social revolution that values generosity and compassion, and, in general, builds a better world and sets an example for our kids.

Because of the great deal of negativity in the news on a daily basis, I want to inspire people to make their own news and feel good about what they do rather than complain and be brainwashed to think everything is bad.

As the initial card holder or *Be You. Be Great.* visionary, you are the first person in the chain. Your random act of kindness and card are passed on to someone (relative, friend, colleague, stranger, etc.) who, hopefully, will keep passing them on. Each card has a unique code and number, and once the card is registered at www.beyoubegreat.net, you will be able to watch how your act of kindness spreads around the world.

Everyone wants to leave a legacy, and this good deed you're about to perform, on a small but compounding scale, allows you to do that.

> **"No act of kindness, no matter how small,
> is ever wasted."**
> **– Aesop**

Your Rewards

Your reward will be twofold. Not only will you have gone seven days without complaining, but you will also have affected someone else's life in a positive way. This challenge, like the rest of the book, is designed to change your life for the better.

Complaining, criticizing, and gossiping will be replaced with positivity and optimism. Negativity assassinates your energy and the hippocampus in your brain, turning your brain into mush. Too much negativity and complaining, and you actually start becoming more sluggish and unproductive, especially in the workplace. No Negatives replaces complaining with finding solutions, generating appreciation, and building better relationships within both your peer group and your workplace.

Let's be honest: you can complain and get frustrated about a lot of things; however, some (if not most) are out of your control. It is simply not worth wasting your mental and emotional energy complaining about things like the weather, the economy, the government, growing older, traffic, and what others say, feel, or do. **Control the controllables** and watch how your life changes for the better.

> **"If you don't like something, change it.**
> **If you can't change it, change your attitude.**
> **Don't complain."**
> **– Maya Angelou**

My Takeaway for this chapter:

Go to www.beyoubegreat.net and download the complimentary No Negatives infographic and place it on your fridge. This will be a great reminder and will keep you on track.

When this challenge seems too tough and you have to start again, remember that it is hard to lead a positive life if you're always complaining.

Chapter 20: Conclusion and Final Thoughts

"To succeed, jump as quickly at
opportunities as you do at conclusions."
– Benjamin Franklin

Jump. Just Do It.

Several people have asked me about the significance of the front cover of this book and what it means or symbolizes. That picture was taken at the top of a 10-meter (32.8-foot) Olympic diving platform on the Gold Coast in Australia. The young man in the picture is a 10-year-old boy with the world at his feet and his life in front of him.

Most of us go through life fearing things and scared of making the wrong decisions.

I wanted people to look at the front cover and ask, "That's a long way up. Will he jump?"

I wanted the viewer to say, "Go ahead, young man, take the leap. Jump. Just do it" – and that is the message I have tried to convey throughout this entire book.

Get out there. Have a go and back yourself. Don't be scared; have faith in your ability. And just do it.

The young boy had no regrets, and he made the jump successfully. He was hesitant to jump, as most of us would be, but when he got out of the pool and had completed what he'd set out to do, he was all smiles and wanted to do it again.

Most of the time, our fear is nothing more than a conditioned response to negative assumptions.

Although the thought of jumping from so high up can feel overwhelming, the fear you build up is not as powerful as it seems. Fear is only as formidable as your mind allows it to be.

You always have control. The key is to acknowledge your fear and directly address it. Get to the top of the diving board and confront it face to face, as the young man did in the cover of this book.

Carpe diem, for this moment may not come again.
– Ritchie Gibson

A Sincere and Heartfelt Thank You.

If you have enjoyed this book, please consider leaving a positive revue and comment either with Amazon or on my website (www.beyoubegreat.net) or even feel free to email me at ritchie@beyoubegreat.net.

I read *every* comment and respond to everyone who takes the time to write to me.

As an author, your feedback is very important and greatly appreciated. Your valued positive reviews are vital in influencing other readers and letting people know you enjoyed this book.

Be sure to check out my website at www.beyoubegreat. net for a complete list of my books, journal and aids to improve your journey through life. My Passport to Success is made up of six separate challenges over a 12 month period and is designed to significantly change lives if you have the will power to stick with it.

Thank you for investing your most valuable asset with me. Your time.

Next time. Best time.

Ritchie Gibson